THE WAY
PEOPLE
LIVE

Life Among the Ibo Women of Nigeria

Titles in The Way People Live series include:

THE WAY
PEOPLE
LIVE

Life Among the Ibo Women of Nigeria

by Salome Nnoromele

Lucent Books, P.O. Box 289011, San Diego, CA 92198-9011

Special thanks to Marie Mitchell,
Carol Hunt, Alan Hunt, and Patrick Nnoromele
for reviewing the drafts of this manuscript
for accuracy of thought and expression

Library of Congress Cataloging-in-Publication Data

Nnoromele, Salome, 1967–
    Life among the Ibo women of Nigeria / by Salome Nnoromele.
       p.   cm. — (The way people live)
    Includes bibliographical references and index.
    Summary: Examines the traditional role of Ibo women as equal partici-
pants in the social, economic, religious, and political lives of their communities and how this role has been influenced and changed by centuries of
colonization and the pressures of modern society.
    ISBN 1-56006-344-0 (lib. bdg. : alk. paper)
    1. Women, Igbo—History—Juvenile literature.   2. Women, Igbo—
Social conditions—Juvenile literature.   3. Igbo (African people)—Social
life and customs—Juvenile literature.   4. Nigeria—Social life and
customs—Juvenile literature. [1. Igbo (African people)—Social life and
customs.   2. Nigeria—Social life and customs.]
I. Title. II. Series.
DT515.45.I33N66   1998

                                      97-45172
                                          CIP
                                            AC

Printed in the U.S.A.

In memory of my brother
Paul Olusegun Momah, 1972–1995

Contents

Discovering the Humanity in Us All

The Way People Live series focuses on pockets of human culture. Some of these are current cultures, like the Eskimos of the Arctic; others no longer exist, such as the Jewish ghetto in Warsaw during World War II. What many of these cultural pockets share, however, is the fact that they have been viewed before, but not completely understood.

To really understand any culture, it is necessary to strip the mind of the common notions we hold about groups of people. These stereotypes are the archenemies of learning. It does not even matter whether the stereotypes are positive or negative; they are confining and tight. Removing them is a challenge that's not easily met, as anyone who has ever tried it will admit. Ideas that do not fit into the templates we create are unwelcome visitors—ones we would prefer remain quietly in a corner or forgotten room.

The cowboy of the Old West is a good example of such confining roles. The cowboy was courageous, yet soft-spoken. His time (it is always a he, in our template) was spent alternatively saving a rancher's daughter from certain death on a runaway stagecoach, or shooting it out with rustlers. At times, of course, he was likely to get a little crazy in town after a trail drive, but for the most part, he was the epitome of inner strength. It is disconcerting to find out that the cowboy is human, even a bit childish. Can it really be true that cowboys would line up to help the cook on the trail drive grind coffee, just hoping he would give them a little stick of pep-

permint candy that came with the coffee shipment? The idea of tough cowboys vying with one another to help "Coosie" (as they called their cooks) for a bit of candy seems silly and out of place.

So is the vision of Eskimos playing video games and watching MTV, living in prefab housing in the Arctic. It just does not fit with what "Eskimo" means. We are far more comfortable with snow igloos and whale blubber, harpoons and kayaks.

Although the cultures dealt with in Lucent's The Way People Live series are often historically and socially well known, the emphasis is on the personal aspects of life. Groups of people, while unquestionably affected by their politics and their governmental structures, are more than those institutions. How do people in a particular time and place educate their children? What do they eat? And how do they build their houses? What kinds of work do they do? What kinds of games do they enjoy? The answers to these questions bring these cultures to life. People's lives are revealed in the particulars and only by knowing the particulars can we understand these cultures' will to survive and their moments of weakness and greatness.

This is not to say that understanding politics does not help to understand a culture. There is no question that the Warsaw ghetto, for example, was a culture that was brought about by the politics and social ideas of Adolf Hitler and the Third Reich. But the Jews who were crowded together in the ghetto cannot be understood by the Reich's politics. Their life was a day-to-day battle for existence, and the creativity and methods they used to prolong their lives is a vital story of human perseverance that would be denied by focusing only on the institutions of Hitler's Germany. Knowing that children as young as five or six outwitted Nazi guards on a daily basis, that Jewish policemen helped the Germans control the ghetto, that children attended secret schools in the ghetto and even earned diplomas—these are the things that reveal the fabric of life, that can inspire, intrigue, and amaze.

Books in The Way People Live series allow both the casual reader and the student to see humans as victims, heroes, and onlookers. And although humans act in ways that can fill us with feelings of sorrow and revulsion, it is important to remember that "hero," "predator," and "victim" are dangerous terms. Heaping undue pity or praise on people reduces them to objects, and strips them of their humanity.

Seeing the Jews of Warsaw only as victims is to deny their humanity. Seeing them only as they appear in surviving photos, staring at the camera with infinite sadness, is limiting, both to them and to those who want to understand them. To an object of pity, the only appropriate response becomes "Those poor creatures!" and that reduces both the quality of their struggle and the depth of their despair. No one is served by such two-dimensional views of people and their cultures.

With this in mind, The Way People Live series strives to flesh out the traditional, two-dimensional views of people in various cultures and historical circumstances. Using a wide variety of primary quotations—the words not only of the politicians and government leaders, but of the real people whose lives are being examined—each book in the series attempts to show an honest and complete picture of a culture removed from our own by time or space.

By examining cultures in this way, the reader will notice not only the glaring differences from his or her own culture, but also will be struck by the similarities. For indeed, people share common needs—warmth, good company, stability, and affirmation from others. Ultimately, seeing how people really live, or have lived can only enrich our understanding of ourselves.

Women in Transition

The history of women in the Ibo society of Nigeria contains two conflicting images. One is of the vibrant, fearless precolonial woman who knew herself and her worth and often claimed equality with men in the community; the other is of the subordinate, confused, but still active, modern woman struggling to define herself in an ever-changing world. Both oral and written accounts by natives as well as nonnatives who visited precolonial Ibo society describe Ibo women as strong, independent-minded people who took full part in the economic, religious, and political lives of their communities. "They have intense vigor and vitality for life," writes Sylvia Leith-Ross, one of the earliest visitors to Iboland. "The women are hard-headed and move fearlessly through the complexities of life."[1] Lord Frederick Lugard, one of Britain's colonial administrators in Nigeria, describes precolonial Ibo women as "ambitious, courageous, self-reliant, hard-working, and independent. [They] claim full equality with the opposite sex, and would seem indeed to be the dominant partner."[2]

The Effects of Colonization

But the lives of Ibo women changed irrevocably when the British invaded and settled Iboland from the beginning of the sixteenth to the mid–twentieth century. "Iboland underwent fundamental transformations in all areas of life under the British control," states Ibo historian Felix K. Ekechi. "Colonization changed the democratic nature of the economic, religious, social, and political institutions in Iboland. It enforced policies that diminished the roles and status of Ibo women, making them second class citizens."[3] Contemporary Ibo women simply describe their lives as "lives in transition," existing somewhere at the crossroads between traditional and newly acquired values. As such, their lives are defined by conflict, confusion, and struggle, as they attempt to find for themselves a comfortable place in society.

Second-Class Citizens

It is true that in comparison to the lives of women in the other major ethnic groups in Nigeria (the Yorubas and the Hausas), modern Ibo women enjoy considerable freedom of thought and of action. For example, Ibo women have always had the right to vote. Both boys and girls have equal access to elementary and secondary education. And almost every girl whose parents can afford it is encouraged to study beyond the high school level.

But freedom to work and vote and access to education do not mean women are equal to men. Jack Harris, an anthropologist, reports that during his field research in Iboland he was repeatedly told by Ibo men "that women are subsidiary to men, that they are practically chattels [slaves], and have no

In an interview with the author, Uchenna Adigha, a twenty-nine-year-old Ibo woman who teaches at a high school in Iboland, tells the story of how she became a literature rather than math or science teacher.

"In secondary school I was good in math and very good in the sciences. But somehow, I got the message that I was not supposed to be good in these subjects. Women and girls are supposed to excel in literature and language arts, not in math or the sciences. So I convinced myself that I did not have to be good in math and the sciences. I focused my studies on literature and language. And that's how I became a literature teacher instead of a math or biology teacher. Or perhaps a scientist."

Modern Ibo women have less freedom than their precolonial counterparts, who enjoyed political power and proclaimed their equality with men.

power other than that allowed them by men."[4] Harris reported his research in 1940, but his findings for the most part hold true, as contemporary Ibo women are denied access to political leadership positions. Currently, they hold less than 1 percent of political offices in Iboland. Even though women have access to higher education, they are proportionally segregated based on gender in terms of what subjects they study, as opposed to men. Women are somehow pressured into studying and training for the so-called women occupations, such as nursing, secretarial work, and primary school teaching. "Far fewer women train for the professions," says Carolyne Dennis, a schoolteacher who has taught in Nigeria for seventeen years. "University statistics show that many women choose to study language arts while men focus on engineering and other science or mathematical science courses."[5]

Economic Restrictions, Financial Hardships

The story is the same in the economic arena. Though Ibo women are expected to work outside the home and contribute financially to the well-being of the family, they are denied access to many economic opportunities. More and more women find themselves economically marginalized and unable to meet their financial domestic duties. Grants for agriculture still go to men—the government chooses to fund large cash crop farmers and ignore the women who mainly grow food crops. Also, an Ibo woman cannot buy or sell land or property without a male representative. "To buy land," states Harris, "a woman needs a male proxy [representative], either her husband or a close male relative. This man retains the title to the land, even though in practice the land is owned by the woman."[6]

Many Ibo women find these restrictions and conflicts annoying and unfair. Some women's organizations are currently working to reinstate what they call "women's positions of lost authority." They believe that reclaiming the past and reinstating traditional rituals and customs, which gave power and status to women in society, will restore balance and bring stability and fulfillment to the lives of present-day Ibo women.

The Ibo Society

The Ibos or Igbos (pronounced "Ee-bohs" or "Eeg-bohs") constitute one of the three major ethnic groups in Nigeria. The others are the Yorubas to the west and the Hausas to the north. The Ibos' ancestral homeland lies in southeastern Nigeria, between the Niger and Cross Rivers. Geographically, it measures about 40,922 square kilometers, with a population estimated at 16 million people.

A Flourishing Rain Forest

Although deforestation, massive erosions, and landslides have changed its current topography, traditional Iboland (from approximately third century B.C. to late nineteenth century) was a flourishing tropical rain forest. "It was considered the belt of the equatorial rainforest,"[7] writes Derry Yakubu, a Nigerian anthropologist. The land was so thickly forested that its earliest European visitors referred to it as "the interior," or "the hinterland." One British traveler at the beginning of the twentieth century noted that "the forest reigned supreme in Iboland. It formed the background of every scene. Homes and gardens and farm and livestock must learn to live and flourish beneath its shade." Palm trees were plentiful, especially in the deep and narrow valleys.

But the general impression was that of magnificent forest trees rising out of a light undergrowth of brush and saplings, with all the varied greens, straight clean tree-trunks and noble branchings.[8]

The Climate

Embedded in the tropical rain forest, traditional Iboland had a very warm climate with two major seasons: wet (*Udu mmiri*) and dry (*Uguru*). The wet months lasted from February to September. The climate was hot and humid during this period. And the air was often muggy from the frequent heavy rainfall. The average annual rainfall was estimated at 105 inches. The dry season, also called the *harmattan*, began in October and ended in January. The weather was chilly in the morning, but the temperature could rise to 80 degrees Fahrenheit by midafternoon. Occasional rain fell during the dry season, but the period was usually dusty and extremely windy. Farmers organized their planting calendar around the seasons. They planted their crops during the rainy season, and harvested and stored their produce during the last months of the rainy season and the early part of the dry season, from September to November. According to G. T. Basden,

Between seasons was considered leisure time. People did craft work, caught up on repairs around the house, and generally rested from all the hard work they had done during the planting or harvesting of crops.[9]

Clothing and Physical Appearance

Living in the intense heat of the tropical climate required that the Ibos wear relatively loose clothing. Boys and girls wore little or no clothes until they reached puberty. The traditional attire for adult men consisted of a loose cotton shirt over an ankle-length wrapper or loincloth. Men always carried a machete, a long, very sharp blade, used to clear forest paths and to defend themselves and their families against dangerous animals living in the forest.

Women's clothing consisted of a blouse and two wrappers of multicolored geometric or floral design. The first wrapper was draped around the body from the waist to the ankle. The second wrapper overlapped the first from the waist to the knees, giving the wrappers a layered look. The blouse was tucked inside the wrapper. The women wore head ties or

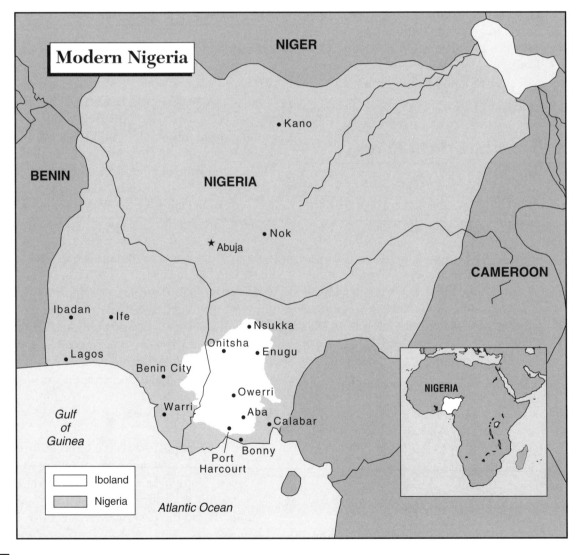

Modern Nigeria

NIGER

BENIN

NIGERIA

• Kano

• Nok

★ Abuja

CAMEROON

Ibadan

• Ife

• Nsukka

Onitsha

• Enugu

Lagos

Benin City

NIGERIA

• Owerri

Warri

Aba

• Calabar

Gulf of Guinea

Bonny

Port Harcourt

Iboland

Nigeria

Atlantic Ocean

Wearing only a loincloth, an Ibo man from Ugwu Eme, Nigeria, dresses in traditional attire.

simply plaited their hair with thread and beads. Earrings, necklaces, and different types of bangles were worn for desired effect. The best way to describe the Ibo traditional attire, says British anthropologist Sylvia Leith-Ross, is "colorful." "The Ibos' natural sense of color is excellent. They can take three pieces of crudely patterned Manchester cloth, glaringly unmatchable, and somehow blend them harmoniously."[10]

The Ibo Language

The Ibos speak variant but mutually understood dialects of the Ibo language, a part of the Kwa group of West African languages. It is an extremely tonal language that depends on pitch, voice inflections, and context for meaning. For example, the word *akwa* could mean four different things, depending on context and which syllable is stressed: "clothes" (*ákwá*), "bed" (*ákwà*), "egg" (*àkwá*), or "to cry" (*àkwà*). "Even though its tonality makes the language difficult for non-natives to learn, it is a rich and musical language," writes Sonia Bleeker, an anthropologist who lived in Iboland for many years. "The Ibo language is very flowery, full of idiomatic and proverbial sayings."[11] Thus the Ibos say *"Ilulu bu manu eji eri okwu"* (Proverbs are oil with which words are eaten). Any speaker who does not know how to apply idioms, proverbs, and myths is said to be a novice, or learner, of

An Ibo student from Onitsha, Nigeria, writes Ibo proverbs on a classroom blackboard. Traditional Ibo society used proverbs to express and teach community values and beliefs.

the language, and any speech without them is dry; the speaker is said to be eating his words (*o na-ata okwu ata*).

Proverbs and idiomatic sayings were significant to traditional Ibo society because they were used to express and transmit community values, beliefs, and attitudes towards life. T. Uzodinma Nwala, an Ibo professor who studies traditional culture and beliefs, states that

from such proverbs as "Otu nkpisi aka ruta manu ozoe ibe ya onu" (when one finger touches oil, it reaches to the rest) and "Nwata kwo aka osoro ndi okenye rie ihe" (when a child washes his hands, he deserves to eat with his elders), we garner that traditional Ibo society valued individual achievement while promoting community spirit.[12]

Individuals were responsible for making their own way in the world. But at the same time, they were fully aware that their actions affected all members of the community. Therefore, one needed to be very careful of one's behavior and decisions.

Village Life

"The Ibos' simultaneous emphasis on individual actions and community living was possible because of the setup of traditional society,"[13] writes anthropologist Simon Ottenberg. The basic unit of the social, economic, and political life of traditional Ibo society was the extended family. Precolonial Ibos lived in clusters of independent villages made up of several patrilineal extended families. The population of each village is estimated to have ranged from a few hundred people to several thousand.

The villages had no king or single ruler to whom others paid homage. In fact, the political, social, and religious life of the village was extremely democratic. Community decisions were made in consultation with every member of the village through established institutions, such as the council of elders, age groups, the council of chiefs, women's associations, and secret societies. Reflecting on the sociopolitical setup of Ibo villages, Henry John, an early visitor to a Niger Ibo village during the nineteenth century, said that he felt he "was in a free land among a free people. True liberty existed in Igboland, though its name was not inscribed on any monument."[14]

Extended Family Compounds

Usually at the center of the village was the village square, a small clearing interspersed with trees, where general meetings and ceremonies were held. Farther from the square were clusters of compounds, or *ezi,* where extended patrilineal families lived. Each was walled with mud or fenced with palm leaves. These compounds were usually fifty to one hundred yards apart with "stretches of forest or farmland in between and a network of winding footpaths. It was possible to be in the heart of a village and not see one vestige of habitation,"[15] writes Leith-Ross.

In a typical compound lived a man and his wife, or wives, unmarried daughters, unmarried sons, and married sons with their families. A man's other relatives, his mother, brothers and their families, and divorced daughters and their children, also lived with him in the compound. "A typical compound, therefore, may have a few individuals to a few hundreds,"[16] notes anthropologist Derry Yakubu.

The structure of the compounds was similar. Each had a circular building at the center, called the *obi.* This served as a meeting place, reception room, and as an eating room during important occasions like festivals or other religious ceremonies. The size and style of the *obi* varied between families, but it was usually a low-roofed mud hut with a carved wood door at its entrance. The *obi* usually contained two mud couches, a bamboo bed, and two or three low wooden stools for household use. Close to the *obi* was a small miniature

Ibo Proverbs

Proverbs are a very important feature of the Ibo language and society. They express the people's view of life and attitude toward things in general. The following proverbs, cited in T. Uzodinma Nwala's book Igbo Philosophy, *are prevalent in daily Ibo conversations and thoughts.*

1. *"Mmadu adighi emecheta ihe oma, ewere ihe ojo kwua ya ugwo."* (It is bad to return evil to a person who has done good.)

2. *"Aka ikpa kwo aka nri, aka nri akwo aka ikpa."* (When the left hand washes the right hand, the right hand in turn washes the left hand.)

3. *"Onye na-amaghi onye toro ya agabeghi."* (He who does not know his elder is not yet mature.)

4. *"Egbe bere, ugo bere, nke si ibe ya ebela nku kwapu ya n'ike."* (Let the kite perch and let the eagle perch; whichever tries to prevent the other from perching, let his wings fall off.)

5. *"Igwe bu ike."* (Multitude is strength.)

house—the shrine of ancestors. This was where the oldest male member of the family poured libations daily to the spirit of the departed ancestors, asking for protection and prosperity for the living.

Individual Dwellings

Sons of the family built their individual houses around the *obi*. If a man had more than one wife, which was an accepted practice among the Ibos at this time, each wife had a house built for her and her children near the husband's house. The houses were rectangular and built of smooth, processed clay bricks. The roofs were made of overlapped palm leaves intricately woven to withstand rain and sun. Small openings were cut in the mud walls to serve as windows. Depending on the size and needs of the family, each house contained two or more rooms.

Like the *obi*, the inside decorations of the houses were simple. There were mud couches and low wooden stools for sitting. The beds were made of either mud or bamboo rods, covered with a goatskin rug or a rush mat. Attached to the houses of the men was a storage house, or *oba*, where men stored their yearly harvest of the Ibo yam. The women's houses had an attached kitchen for cooking and storing food crops other than yam, such as maize and cocoyams. At the back of the compound was a little building that housed a pit latrine for all family members' use. A bathing place was also erected slightly behind the houses.

One early European visitor to Iboland noted that "Ibo villages were models of cleanliness and good building and their farms were kept the same way." [17] Another visitor said, "As we passed through the village, we were struck with its clean well-kept houses and roads. The people certainly take a great pride in having their homes nice." [18] These accounts are true, says Elizabeth Isichei, an Ibo historian. "The Ibos took pride in maintaining and keeping their dwellings clean." [19]

The yards both inside and outside the compound were swept daily and weeded regularly. At the edge of the compound were garden plots where vegetables and other crops were grown. Usually a cluster of palm trees, as well as mango, orange, and other fruit trees, stood in the compound to provide shade, which people sat under to play games, do chores, make crafts, or prepare meals.

This shade also provided a good site for the informal teaching and acculturation of

In Human Terms

Traditional Ibos had strong, intimate ties with one another. Living in large, extended family compounds assured that a person was always loved, nurtured, and encouraged. Sonia Bleeker, an anthropologist who studied traditional Ibo ways of life for many years, describes this essential communal spirit in her book, The Ibo of Biafra.

"At home, in the compound, a person is always surrounded by relatives. He has their cooperation, their affection, their encouragement, and their teaching and guidance. The obligations he has towards them make him feel wanted and needed in the happy community. When he is sick, his relatives come and stay with him till he recovers. When it is time for him to marry, his relatives contribute to the bridewealth [dowry] and come with gifts to celebrate his wedding. They fill the compound with gaiety and good will."

Traditional Ibo kitchens were attached to the women's houses. Here, family members prepare a pit fire on the floor of their kitchen while a bundle of corn hangs overhead.

Ibo boys and girls. G. T. Basden, an archbishop in Iboland for thirty-five years, states that "sitting under the trees, helping parents perform various household tasks, children learn the rules of behavior and community values." Parents told their children stories and passed on important family and village histories.

By the time young people arrived at the age of puberty, they have learned all they can learn from their daily contacts with life, certainly as much as their own folks were capable of teaching them.[20]

Collective Responsibility

Living together in large extended families made traditional Ibos a close-knit people. It also created a sense of collective responsibility. "Community spirit is very strong among the Igbo," writes Ibo anthropologist Victor Uchendu. "Almost from the first, the individual is aware of his dependence on his kin group and his community. He also realizes the necessity of making his own contribution to the group to which he owes so much."[21] Consequently, everyone, males, females, and children, had important roles to play in maintaining the well-being of the family. For example, the oldest male member of the family served as the spiritual head and the ultimate authority figure. His role was to maintain law and order in the family, pour libations at the shrine of the ancestors, and represent the family's interests in the larger village community.

Children were expected to help care for their younger siblings and run errands for older members of the family. It was also their duty to obtain firewood for cooking and to fetch water from local streams. Men and women had complementary tasks. "Men did hard labor, such as clearing the land for farming, cultivating, planting, and harvesting crops. They did home constructions and repairs," [22] writes Yakubu. The women helped men in farming, weeding, harvesting, and processing farm products. They were also responsible for supervising and disciplining the children, making sure they grew up to be useful citizens. Women performed most of the household work as well, including housekeeping and preparation of meals. An Ibo man, reminiscing over life in the communal-based traditional Ibo society, said,

> we were all habituated to labor from our earliest years. Everyone contributed something to the common stock, and as we were unacquainted with idleness, we had no beggars. Practically no one, except the very young and very old, were exempt from manual work. Productivity and hard work were highly esteemed. [23]

Native Food

The Ibos' native diet consisted primarily of pounded yam, cassava, or cocoyam (*fufu*) served with seasoned vegetable soup made with sun-dried or smoked fish or meat. Foodstuff, such as maize, beans, peanuts, plantains, pumpkins, breadfruit, and okra, was also eaten for variety. Wild and domestic fruits, such as oranges, mangoes, guava, and papaw, were abundant, but they were eaten primarily as snacks and did not form part of the staple diet. Although they raised livestock (chicken, goats, and sheep), the traditional Ibo preferred dried fish over meat. And "bush meat" (hunted meat) was considered more tasty than meat from domestic animals.

In most families, meals were prepared together and everybody ate at the same time. In others, however, each wife was responsible for preparing meals for herself and her children. The wives then took turns preparing the husband's meal. Before eating, the father would offer a portion of his meal and drink to the cult of the ancestors. He thanked them for the meal and for life, and asked for protection from enemies and evil forces. This gesture of honoring the spirit of the dead by regularly offering them libations and asking for protection reflects the Ibo people's profound belief in the power of supernatural forces to affect and determine their life experiences.

Religion

"The Ibos were nothing if not profoundly religious," says Elizabeth Isichei, a scholar of Ibo culture and society. "All accounts of their life reflect that fact." [24] A German missionary to Iboland in 1841 commented how the Ibos believed that everything in their society was governed by gods and ancestors:

> To the Ibo the secular and the sacred, the natural and the supernatural, are a continuum. Supernatural forces continually impinge on life and must be propitiated by appropriate prayers and sacrifices. [25]

Traditional Ibo attitudes toward the supernatural are understandable, says T. Nwala, if one recognizes that the Ibos lived constantly with the harsh realities of their natural environment. They accepted the limitations of human efforts and acknowledged that there were forces higher than humans that helped determine their fate. "Igbo religious life," he states, "is an integral element of their total cultural life which aims at self-realization of some sort that consists in nothing other than living in harmony with the cosmic order." [26]

Belief in Many Gods

The Ibos, like people in most African societies, were polytheists. They believed in and worshiped many gods. Their belief system consisted of three hierarchical layers of the supernatural world. At the head of the hierarchy was the ultimate supernatural being, known as Chukwu (the Great God), or Chineke (God, the Creator). Underneath Chukwu were the lesser but powerful gods, Umuagbara. Below the gods were the spirits of dead ancestors, Ndi Ichie, and the personal gods, Chi.

To the Ibos, the reason for having this hierarchy of the supernatural was quite simple. The people believed that Chukwu was so powerful and so fearful that ordinary human beings could not possibly approach him directly with impunity. To approach Chukwu, one needed the help of the lesser but powerful gods and one's departed ancestors to act as intermediaries.

Umuagbara

The lesser gods consisted of male and female deities with certain specified areas of natural control that often overlapped, including the

The Ibo Worldview

The Ibos believed that the universe was made up of two worlds: the world of humans and the world of spirits. The two worlds are related and interdependent. As Victor Uchendu explains in his book The Igbo of Southeast Nigeria, *the two worlds function on the principle of "beneficial reciprocity."*

"The Igbo world is a 'real' one in every respect. There is the world of man peopled by all created beings and things, both animate and inanimate. The spirit world is the abode of the creator, the deities, the disembodied and malignant spirits, and the ancestral spirits. It is the future abode of the living after their death. There is constant interaction between the world of man and the dead; the visible and invisible forces. Existence for the Igbo, therefore, is a dual but interrelated phenomenon involving the interaction between the material and the spiritual, the visible and the invisible, the good and the bad, the living and the dead."

gods of thunder, the river, the harvest, and so on. These gods were collectively called Agbala, Agbara, Ajala, or Arusi (the oracle). All the gods were respected, but they were not given equal importance and power. Generally, every village recognized one deity as the most powerful depending on the needs and experiences of the community. This deity became the most influential god to the people and occupied a central position in their lives and activities. The deity was believed to control harvest yields, fertility, and life—areas paramount to the survival of a community. Ala or Ani (the earth goddess), was the sacred deity

Ornate sculptures call attention to an Ibo shrine along the road from Nsukka to Enugu, Nigeria. Traditional Ibos practice a polytheistic religion and devote shrines to the various deities they worship.

in some villages. In others, it was Amadioha (the god of thunder) or perhaps the river god, if the village was near the coast.

Libations and prayers were offered daily to the gods. And each village set apart certain periods of the year to feast and make merriment in honor of their gods. "During the feasts, sacrifices and offerings were made as thanksgiving, petitions for protection, absolution for sins, and requests for life, health, children, wealth and security,"[27] notes Nwala. Among the great village festivals or feasts in Iboland were the New Yam Festival (Ifejioku or Iwaji) and the New Year Festival (Igu Aro).

Ndi Ichie and Chi

Beneath the nature gods were the spirits of dead ancestors (Ndi Ichie) and the guardian or personal gods (Chi). The Ibos worshiped their ancestors. They believed that dead ancestors helped protect living relations, prevent them from harm, and intercede for them in times of trouble.

The Chi, or personal god, was believed to be responsible for individual safety and success. It was common for individuals, especially children, to wear talismans or charms (*Ikenga*) as outward symbols of their Chi. No two Chi were alike, and the Ibos believed that one cannot be greater than one's Chi. The views are expressed in numerous proverbs, such as *"Ebe onye dara obu chi ya kwaturu ya"* (Where a person falls, that is where his or her Chi brings him or her down) and *"Chi onye adighi nizu, onwu adighi egbu ya"* (Unless a person's Chi agrees, death does not kill him or her).

It was very unfortunate indeed for an individual to have a lazy or an uncoordinated Chi. This meant consistent failure and poverty. A person who had a history of misfortune was spoken of as *onye chi ojo* (a person with a bad Chi). And when an individual seemed to exist in a perpetual state of misery and misfortune, he or she was advised to die and go ask for a better Chi (*Nwua ga jugharia*).

Reincarnation

"Telling a person to die was not a sign of meanness by the Ibos," explains Nwala. "It merely indicated a belief in reincarnation and the notion that death was not final."[28] The Ibos saw death as a transient phase into another life. When a person died, the individual was believed to continue his or her life in the spirit world. As Victor Uchendu, an Ibo ethnographer, explains, "The world of the dead is a world full of activities; its inhabitants manifest in their behavior and thought processes that they are 'living.'"[29] Life in the world of the dead, however, was viewed as temporary. The dead were eventually reincarnated after they had been given the opportunity to determine their future fate in the world of humans. It was, therefore, of paramount importance that a balance be maintained

The Ibo Deities or Nature Gods

The Ibos believed that the natural world was controlled by supernatural forces. T. Uzodinma Nwala indicates in his book Igbo Philosophy *that every aspect of nature had a god associated with it.*

"The nature of the local deities, oracles, and abstract forces and ancestral spirits reflect the nature of the traditional Igbo society and its environment as well as the ideals cherished by the various communities. The deities are associated with the natural environment such as rivers, trees, climate, topography and the natural elements. River deities are found in the riverine areas, and they answer the names of the local rivers associated with them. Thus we have Idemili, Imoh, Otankpa, Ulasi, etc. The frequent electrical storms which endanger life yields belief in the god of Thunder—Amadioha or Kama. Being an agricultural people with much concern for the fertility of the soil, there is general belief in the Earth deity Ala, and Ahajioku or Ifejioku. Thus, Igbo traditional physical environment very much determined the nature of the local deities."

An Ibo priest performs a ritual dance with a group of children in Onitsha, Nigeria. In addition to conducting ceremonies and rituals, priests help to maintain a balance between the Ibo world and the spirit realm.

between the two cosmic orders (the world of humans and the world of spirits) for the well-being of everyone.

Priests and Priestesses

Maintaining the balance between the worlds of humans and spirits was the duty of everyone, with the help of the village priests and priestesses. The chief priest or priestess was in charge of the ceremonies and rituals pertaining to the gods. Priesthood was consid-

ered a special gift from the gods and was usually hereditary. A son or daughter could inherit the gift from a parent. To traditional Ibos, a priest and a priestess were equal, and the words of the gods that the priest or priestess presented were unquestionable and binding.

Diviners

In addition to the priests and priestesses of the gods, there were also male and female diviners, known to the people as *ndi dibia afa*. Since the Ibos believed that everything in life—death, sickness, birth, wealth, and the like—was controlled in the supernatural sphere, the diviners consulted the spirit world for individuals seeking knowledge of the future, the outcome of a journey, or the right time or need to perform a particular task.

Similar to the powers of priesthood, divination was believed to be a gift and could be inherited from a parent or a close relation. A village could have anywhere from three to ten diviners. People consulted their village diviners as well as diviners in other villages. It was not unusual for an Ibo man or woman to travel a great distance to consult a diviner whose fame and gift of divination was well known.

Because of the emphasis on skill and the power of inheritance, women could assume positions of religious authority in the traditional Ibo community. Female priests were given the same respect and rights as male priests. The respect for diviners, consulted equally by men and women, was based on talent, not gender. Thus, women played a significant role in the leadership of Ibo society.

2 Women of Power

Although traditional Ibo society favored men, mainly because the family name and property were carried on through male descendants, the Ibos still recognized and valued the contributions women made to the community. They recognized the differences between men and women and the fact that their needs were often not identical. As such, they created two different powerful and autonomous political systems that handled the affairs of men and women separately. Consequently, men had their own political institutions where they managed and discussed issues affecting them and women had their own separate and equally powerful political institutions through which they managed their affairs.

The Women's Political Organization

Kaneme Okonjo, an Ibo who has studied past and present-day Ibo societies and the role of women in them, states, "We can label such systems of organization 'dual sex' systems, for within them each sex managed its own affairs and women's interests were represented at all levels." Having two political institutions that were considered equal and free ensured that women could organize themselves and carry out their responsibilities without fear of meddling or opposition from the men. It also meant that "women achieved status and recognition not by doing 'men's work' as per-

tains in the Western world, but by working within their own women's group." [30]

The women's political organization paralleled that of the men. It consisted of the main Women's Council, also known as the General Assembly, and different levels of women's associations, known as *Otu* or *Ogbo*, which often served as interest groups for their members. Membership was on the basis of age, marriage, or social status.

The Women's Council

The Women's Council was the central governing body for the women. Meetings were called whenever an issue requiring general or immediate attention arose. It was mandatory that each lineage or extended family be represented at every meeting. As such, the women of a lineage usually appointed a delegate to represent them.

The delegates were accompanied by other lineage women who were free and willing to attend. "The exceptions were pregnant or nursing women because members did not want the meeting disturbed or interrupted by crying babies or a woman in labor," [31] writes researcher Sylvia Leith-Ross. The meetings were held in the village square, an empty space in the marketplace, or in a member's house, if her compound was large enough to accommodate everyone. It was a great honor to hold a meeting in one's home or compound; many wealthy women competed for such an honor, providing food and refreshments for women attending the meeting. Men were not welcome at the women's gatherings.

The Leader of the Women

The Women's Council meetings were chaired by the leader of the women. In some communities, she was called the Omu (the great mother). In others, she was called Ogene Nyanya, or simply *Onye isi umunwanyi* (the women's leader). "The women's leader was often one of the oldest and most respected members of the female community," says historian Kaneme Okonjo. "The office was attained by merit; it was not hereditary."[32]

The leader's other duties included performing certain community ceremonies, disciplining the women of the community, representing the female population in the larger village meetings, and advising women in times of personal conflict or family crises. Okonjo explains:

Because of these invaluable responsibilities, the Omu's qualifications included having good sense and good character, possessing the ability to speak well, a persuasive personality and some degree of wealth.

These leadership skills were important since she did not rule by issuing commands or making decrees.

Her authority rested in her ability to reach a consensus with the women of the community on all issues and on her skills at negotiating with the men on issues that affected all members of the community.[33]

The Women Advisers

The women's leader ruled the women and represented their interests to the larger community with the advice and help of a select group of women known as Ilogo, or Otu

Separate but Equal

The political setup of traditional Ibo society functioned along gender lines. Men and women had separate political institutions; women's organizations paralleled those of the men and were considered as powerful. In her essay "Recovering Igbo Traditions," philosopher Nkiru Nzegwu describes how the system worked.

"The political culture of the Igbos could be theoretically described as dual-sex. Under this structure, women had their own Governing Councils—Ikporo-Onitsha, Nd'inyom— to address their specific concerns and needs as women. The councils protected women's social and economic interests, and guided the community's development. The dual-symmetrical structure accorded immense political profile to women. . . . The socio-political structure required and depended on the active participation of women in the community life. Their views were deemed critical, not because they were women, but because of the special insight they brought to issues by virtue of their spiritual, market and trading duties and their maternal roles."

A *modern Ibo chief displays the traditional dress of the women's leader. Considered the Omu, or great mother, the women's leader attained her position through merit rather than heredity.*

Ogene. These women advisers consisted of the most prominent women in the village—women who, like the women's leader, came from prestigious and respected families. They were also known for having good character and good sense, having achieved high status and wealth through hard work, and for possessing the ability to speak well and not be easily intimidated. As one Ibo woman, Ulunwa Odimba-Nwaru, describes,

> The qualifications of both the women's leader and members of her advisory board

show that traditional Ibos rank eloquence, diligence and good sense as three of the most significant prerequisites to social and political authority and the good life.[34]

Spiritual and Protective Leaders

Most villages regarded the Omu and members of her cabinet as *Ndi amuma* (prophets and seers). According to Ikenna Nzimiro, an Ibo professor of sociology and anthropology, "they were said to dream of spirits who come to them warning of dangers and demanding certain rituals." Consequently, the women performed seasonal rituals aimed at driving evil away from their villages. They prepared special charms to ensure the safety and well-being of all persons attending the market-place. The charms were also meant to ensure market expansion by attracting traders and goods from other areas and preventing market disorder. "In this way, the Omu and members of her cabinet served as spiritual and protective leaders of the entire community."[35]

Before the Cock Crowed

Whenever a special meeting was called or a regular meeting was scheduled, it was the responsibility of the Omu or her representative to call the women together. Very early in the morning on the day of the meeting, before the cock crowed to signal the beginning of a new day and all was quiet, the women's leader took her *Ogene* or *ekwe* (gong), and walked through the village. She beat the gong in a special way as she announced the time and place of the meeting, to which everyone listened carefully. One Ibo woman explains:

Using the Ogene as a tool for communicating messages was such a part of the Ibo traditional life that whenever the gong beat, people stopped whatever they were doing and paid attention. The message preceding the gong beat could be a matter of life and death for the people. So they listened.[36]

An Ibo marketplace on the banks of the Niger River in Onitsha, Nigeria, bustles with activity. Traditionally, the Omu and her advisers supervised the female-dominated markets and worked to ensure their prosperity.

At the meeting, the women's leader and her advisers would present the topics to be discussed. These could range from news of a recent threat to the life of the community to mundane topics such as keeping the markets clean, clearing the paths leading to the markets, and determining rules of market behavior, prices for commodities, and fines for those who violated the rules or failed in their responsibilities. Issues relating to men's village responsibilities were also discussed, such as directing and disciplining young men, clearing forest paths, and performing necessary repairs to public buildings.

"A Case Forbids No One"

Every adult female attending the women's meetings was entitled to speak on any or all of the issues presented for discussion, as long as she had something to say that the others considered worth listening to. As the Ibos say, "A case forbids no one." Any woman was free to completely disagree with others' views or offer a different perspective on the issues. "Other delegates, however, considered it their responsibility to shout down, dismiss, or completely ignore somebody whom they deemed a trouble-maker or 'an idiot,'"[37] states historian Margaret Green. Decisions reached at the meetings were by majority consensus. And because of the respect given to the council, resolutions were binding on everyone in the community, male and female alike.

The women delegates had the responsibility of passing on the decisions to the women who could not attend the meeting and also to the men, if the rules affected them. The women's leader and her cabinet considered it their duty to make everyone comply with the rules. "Although men were not allowed to attend or participate in the women's deliberations, they rarely ever questioned the decisions reached by the women," states anthropologist Sylvia Leith-Ross. This may be partly due to the fact that they trusted the integrity of the women. They also knew that the

The Mother of the Community

In his article "The Political Institutions," Kaneme Okonjo cites an interview he conducted with a newly installed Omu of Obamkpa, a community that is currently trying to revive traditional Ibo values.

"My child [speaking to Okonjo], the Obi is the head of the men, and I am the head of the women. I and my cabinet represent the women in any important town gatherings and deliberations. If decisions arrived at are such that the womenfolk are to be told about them, I get a woman [onye oga] to sound the gong [ekwe] to assemble the women. On less important occasions, my cabinet members pass the word around among the women by word of mouth.

If there is drought, we curse whoever caused it. If there is sickness and people are dying, my cabinet goes naked in the night with live brands to curse whoever brought it. If there is sickness next door [in a neighboring community], I do something with my cabinet to insure that sickness does not enter this town. There are medicines we make at the entrance to the town. These are just a few of my duties. I am the mother of the people, you know, and I have to insure in any way I can that they enjoy continued good health and happiness."

women wished to preserve the peace of the village because it enabled them to carry on their trading. "The men seem also to think that the women have a greater sense of abstract justice,"[38] says Leith-Ross.

Ritual Sanctions

Failure to comply with the resolutions made by the Women's Council brought the women's wrath upon the individual. The women used several community-sanctioned methods, such as strikes, boycotts, or the ritual of "sitting on a man" to force people to comply. The power and success of these methods of enforcement required absolute solidarity from all the women. Jack Harris illustrates this through a story about a woman who refused to pay a fine that the Women's Council had imposed.

> All the women refused to speak to her, to buy from her, or sell to her in the market, or to give her live embers for her fire. Within three weeks of the boycott, the errant woman paid her fine with much pleading and apologies to the entire women's community.[39]

In another incident in which the Women's Council repeatedly asked the men to order some of their members to clean an overgrown path to their farms and repair a bridge, "the men neglected to do this and the women refused to cook food for their husbands until this order was carried out."[40]

Sitting on a Man

When a man violated the rules of the Women's Council, the women sometimes used the ritual known as "sitting on a man" to force

A Greater Sense of Abstract Justice

In her book African Women: A Study of the Ibo of Nigeria, *Sylvia Leith-Ross, an anthropologist who lived among the Ibos for several years, asked the men how they felt about the Women's Council and the decisions they reached at their meetings.*

"The men, although not allowed to attend the council meetings, approved of them and wished the women to keep their power. They trust the integrity of the women in the matter of bribes more than their own. They also know that the women wish to preserve the peace of the town as it enables them to carry on their trading, and they seem also to think that the women have a greater sense of abstract justice. They would not be biased by personal prejudice and long-standing feuds as much as the men."

the individual to comply. Sitting on a man meant "making his life miserable." This often included destroying his property, calling him names, and singing songs that questioned his manhood.

The man being "sat on" could defend himself, if he thought he was up to it. He could ask his relatives to help him defend himself. They could attack the women verbally and issue threats, but they were forbidden from harming the women physically. If they tried, the whole community levied severe punishments on the man and his relatives and could ostracize them from the community. "The authority and immunity given to the women while 'sitting on a man' come from the feeling of respect the Ibos bear their mothers," states Margaret Green.

"One can always hear men dismiss some of the 'outrages' committed by women with the phrase—'Obu Umunwanyi nwe anyi' (It is the women who own us)."[41] Women defended themselves by invoking the power and sanctity of motherhood and their role as food producers. Collectively, says anthropologist Jack Harris

> during strikes, boycotts, or sitting on a man, the women assume the role of Ibo womanhood and [are], in effect, saying: "It is we women who give birth to men. It is we women who feed them. How dare you do an injustice to a woman."[42]

The Women's Associations

Working hand in hand with the Women's Council were the interest groups or women's associations. Issues affecting only a small section of the female population were not handled by the General Assembly, except in cases of extreme altercations among the people involved or when the council felt compelled to intervene for the peace of the community. Minor or individual problems were handled within several established women's organizations, each of which played a different vital role in the community. There were four major groups: Ndi Lolo (titled women), Otu Umuada (daughters of the lineage), Ndi'nyom (wives of the lineage), and Umuagbogho or Umuegbede (the young, unmarried daughters of the lineage).

Titled Women

"Title holding or Ichi ozo in Iboland was the highest social status a man or woman could attain through diligence and hard work,"

In traditional Ibo society, female citizens were governed by the Women's Council and the various women's associations.

states Professor Ikenna Nzimiro. "Ichi ozo in effect tells the entire village community that an individual deserves recognition and respect."[43] Therefore, titles were nontransferable and nonhereditary. One had to earn it.

There were three major ways women could obtain a title. A village could pull its resources together and confer a title on a woman in appreciation of the work she had performed for the community. Children could bestow a title on their mother to show their appreciation and love. Finally, a prosperous woman, with many descendants, could register and legitimize her success by taking a title. "Title holding rites of passage were both rigorous, expensive and arduous,"[44] notes historian Elizabeth Isichei. The ritual involved, among other things, paying a huge fee to the members of the club and providing elaborate entertainment and food to all members of the village on the day of the ceremony. Thus, few women were willing to undertake the task on their own.

"Women who took titles, either as a result of community or individual effort, were considered political and social elites,"[45] says Nzimiro. They were considered leaders and given great respect. When they spoke, everybody listened. The women's leader and members of her cabinet almost always came from this distinguished association. Women title holders were called Ndi Lolo. To indicate their achievement, they wore a special red cap and locally made stone anklets and necklaces, and they carried a fan. "Titled women were recognized anywhere by their appearance,"[46] notes one historian.

Daughters of the Lineage

The Otu Umuada represented the most powerful women's group in a lineage, consisting of all married daughters of the lineage. Even though traditional Ibo society was patrilocal (all daughters were expected to marry and move to their husband's community), women still retained rights and responsibilities in their birth communities. As such, every married Ibo woman had two homes—one in her village of birth, the other in her married community. She visited her birth home regularly bringing gifts and, sometimes, information from her married home. The Umuada had special prerogatives by virtue of their dual homes. Explains Nzimiro:

They acted as diplomats between the two communities of relationship, as ambassadors of good will for their birth communities, and, in times of crises, as

informants against their places of marriage. . . . The Umuada's allegiance were almost always with their fathers' home. Most women would rather divorce their husbands and return home than betray the interests of their place of birth.[47]

Strong allegiance to their places of birth made Umuada "resident outsiders" in their husband's home. But it gave them great influential authority within their natal homes. A brother was not permitted to get married without first informing and receiving the approval of the Umuada. The Umuada were also called upon to settle disputes within the

Although Ibo women relocate to their husband's homes after marriage, they retain rights and responsibilities in their natal communities. These women are known as the Otu Umuada, or daughters of the lineage.

family, especially those between brothers or between a brother and his wife. Even though their decisions were nonbinding, few family members dared to go against their wishes. "The wrath of the Umuada often burned long and deep. It had a way of making, through sanctions and boycotts, the life of any offender miserable,"[48] says Nzimiro.

Wives of the Lineage

The reciprocal group to the Umuada was the Otu Ndi'nyom, representing the interests of the wives of the lineage. Ndi'nyom, by virtue of their position as wives, had less power than the Umuada, but they always maintained their rights and protested to the Omu (the women's leader) whenever they thought the Umuada were too demanding or were encroaching upon their rights. The Omu had the power to intervene and maintain justice and balance between the two groups. Otu Ndi'nyom was also a self-help group. Members looked out for each other's interests. Collectively, they lent money for trading, and shared planting crops with women who may be less fortunate. For the most part, the association helped its members to succeed and lead productive lives.

Unmarried Daughters of the Lineage

The Otu Umuagbogho was the least powerful of the women's groups. It was made up of unmarried young women from the age of twelve and above. "It was mainly a socializing institute for teenagers. Group members learned different traditional dances and rules of social behavior; life-time friendships were also formed,"[49] explains Nzimiro. Politically, they had certain rights and responsibilities and could appeal to either the Umuada or Ndi'nyom when they thought their interests were not being represented. When this attempt failed, they appealed to the Omu for redress.

Having these levels of political organization with specified powers, areas of jurisdiction, and clearly defined appeal processes ensured that the interests of most women in traditional Ibo society were represented. It also meant that women had the opportunity, the freedom, and the access to contribute to the well-being of their society. After studying the character of the Ibo political setup, historian Elizabeth Isichei concluded that "the Ibo political system may not have been one hundred percent democratic but it came very close to it."[50]

3 Women's Work

"Ibo women have always worked. They grow up in their villages with self-confidence and courage, knowing that they can always support themselves and their children. Even if a husband is generous and wealthy, his wives are expected to work all the same,"[51] states anthropologist Sonia Bleeker.

Women's work in traditional Ibo society, therefore, meant that in addition to cooking, housework, and taking care of the children, women were expected to work outside the home and to make economic contributions to the well-being of their families.

The wife's contribution to the needs of the household was direct and indispensable. According to G. T. Basden, an Iboland archbishop, "Women who worked hard were appreciated and a husband showed his appreciation of the wife's services by giving her a present occasionally, usually in the form of a wrapper [an article of clothing]."[52] Conversely, a woman who was not considered aggressive in the workplace was believed to be lazy. She was called Mmiri Oyi (cold water), disrespected, and became the laughingstock of the village. People used her as an example of what happened to people who did not work hard.

The economy of traditional Ibo society was predominantly agricultural. The Ibos were subsistence farmers. Each family grew most of the food it needed to survive. Consequently, in order to meet their economic responsibilities, most Ibo women combined farming and trading. "Fieldwork and marketing filled the Ibo women's days fairly well," says Sylvia Leith-Ross. "Those living on the banks of River Niger or the Cross River combined farmwork, marketing and fishing."[53] Women also did one form of craft or another in between the planting and harvesting seasons.

Fishing

Since the majority of the Ibos lived inland, where big rivers were absent, most of them did not fish. Fishing was left solely to those who lived near these rivers. The Ibos called them ndi mba mmiri (people of the water areas). In these communities, both men and women fished actively.

The method of fishing varied, depending on the season. During the dry season, from October to January, the most popular method of fishing consisted of "draining local streams and ponds until they were only about one-foot deep."[54] Women then used nets and baskets to gather the trapped fish. At other times of the year, people fished in big rivers. They used dugout canoes, traveling about two to three miles from land. "Then they used home made baskets, small throw nets, gill nets, cast nets, and drift nets of different meshes to trap and catch the fish,"[55] explains anthropologist Barry Floyd. An average catch per canoe per day was estimated at 46.5 pounds, normally consisting of crabs, prawns, crayfish, catfish, tilapia, sardines, oysters, and bonga.

Since traditional Ibo society had no method of refrigeration, most products were eaten fresh or dried for preservation. A family usually kept a good portion of their catch for their needs. The rest were air dried or smoked and then taken to the market and sold to traders from inland villages.

Farming

For men and women who lived in the coastal areas and those who lived inland, farming formed a large part of their lives. Everyone held and cultivated land. However, while everybody—male and female—was expected to farm, the Ibos made a distinction between crops men could grow and the ones women could grow. They also differentiated between the types of farm activities women could and could not participate in.

A primary farming duty of the men was planting the Ibo yam (*ji*), a big fibrous tuber that sometimes measured two feet long and weighed up to one hundred pounds. The men were also responsible for "clearing and preparing the farmlands, cutting stakes and training the yam vines as well as building the yam barns and tying the harvest," states Daryll Forde, an ethnographer. "Men also cut the palm fruits, tapped and sold palm wine and the palm oil which the women prepare."[56] Women processed palm oil from palm fruits. They weeded and tended the men's farms during the growing season and also helped to bring the crops home during harvest.

On their own farms, which were often closer to home than those of the men, women could plant anything but the yam. As Leith-Ross explains, "This in reality meant that the women were responsible for growing the larger part of the food stuff and for feeding the family for the greater part of the year

With the aid of a vine rope, an Ibo man climbs a palm tree to harvest its valuable nuts. Ibo culture relies heavily on the palm nut, extracting its oil and making wine from its fruit.

when yams grown by the men were no longer available."[57] Women's crops included cassava, maize, beans, cocoyams, peanuts, tomatoes, peppers, okra, and other green-leafed vegetables. They also raised the livestock that provided much of the meat in the Ibo diet.

It is difficult to find a sufficient reason for the division of labor among the Ibos. Some argue that it indicates the paradox in Ibo village life in which women were given authority over some things but not over others. However, some scholars argue that the reason for the division of labor was simple. "The cocoyams and other food stuffs were easier to grow than the yam and they did not require as much space," says an Ibo writer. "Consequently, while the cocoyams, maize, peppers, tomatoes, and the cassava were planted on farms nearer to the homes, yams were often planted in far away larger and more fertile farms."[58] This made it possible for women to work on the farm and keep an eye on the home when men traveled to the faraway farms. Having women's farms nearer to the homes also gave women quick access to their crops. However, women were required to accompany the men to their farms when the yams needed weeding and during harvest. Many people were needed to carry the yams home from the farm.

Crafts

Usually after harvesting and storing the farm crops, the Ibos spent the nonplanting season, from November to February, making crafts. "Pre-colonial Ibo society achieved highly developed handicrafts in weaving, pottery-making, smithing, wood carving etc.,"[59] writes Uzodinma Nwala, an Ibo philosopher and historian. Metalworking and wood carving were men's work. The men made outstanding forms of masks, statuettes, stools, chip-carved doors and panels, as well as different types of brass and copper anklets and bracelets. The masks and chip carvings had geometrical designs composed of hatching, cross-hatching, lozenges, circles, and quatrefoils. Some of the designs had personal meanings, but most expressed elements of spirituality and the people's conception of life, such as the relationship between humans and their environment and between humans and the gods.

Women concentrated mainly on making pottery and weaving cloth, mats, and baskets. Their work, however, was as outstanding and as skillful as the men's. Ibo women excelled in weaving, notes an Ibo historian. "When our women were not employed with the men in tillage, their usual occupation was spinning and weaving cotton, which they afterwards dyed and made into excellent garments,"[60] he writes. The cloth woven by the women was elaborately patterned and colorful. Referring specifically to the cloth made by the Akwette Ibo community, a visitor to Iboland says, "The southern Ibo town of Akwette made textiles

A Subsistence Economy Based on Sexual Division of Labor

Traditional Ibo society emphasized division of labor based on gender. In his book Igbo Philosophy, *T. Uzodinma Nwala explains how the economic division of labor worked in precolonial Ibo society.*

"Traditional Igbo society is predominantly an agricultural society with subsistence farming in all corners of the society. The main crops grown include yam, cassava, maize, rice, cocoyam. Certain areas, as a result of soil fertility, produce more than others or rather are noted for certain crops. Palm products are also an important feature of the economy. There is specialization or division of labor according to sex. Men plant yams, climb palm trees and tap wine; they also clear and prepare the land, cut stakes, train the yam vines, build barns and tie the harvest. Women plant their own varieties of crops (cocoyam, maize, groundnut, okra, pepper, etc.), weed and carry in the yams from the farm. They also press the palm fruits to produce oil and kernel."

(Right) An Ibo sculptor and his assistant carve an elaborate mask out of a tree trunk they cut in a nearby forest. (Below) A wooden statuette, crafted for use in a shrine, is an outstanding example of Ibo art.

so superb that imported cloth could not rival them."[61] The textiles were initially made from bark fiber. Later, probably by mid–nineteenth century, cotton weaving was introduced as a result of contact with the outside world. As early as the 1850s, a missionary noted that every woman in Iboland wove cloth from "the cotton which grows on the trees in abundance, and they do it so beautifully."[62]

Ibo women and girls also had a fondness for beads, trinkets, and ivory necklaces and bangles. "Fashion varied. Ear and hair ornaments were very popular, as well as waist beads—nkpulu-ife, or jigida," writes one historian. Some of the beads the women made and wore had certain spiritual and cultural attachments. For example, the waist beads, a string of black, round beads of a particular pattern and design, could only be worn by married or affianced women. "The waist beads must never be removed while a woman's husband was alive."[63] To remove the waist beads suggested a woman's discontent with her married life and a readiness to ask for a divorce. Small wrist beads were also worn by women and girls as charms.

Markets

Most crafts made by the Ibos—pottery, mats, beads, masks, carved doors, and so on—were kept for family use. Others, however, were sold with surplus crops in the market either for a profit or in exchange for something a family needed. Traditional Ibo villages considered the marketplace part of the women's sphere. Richard Henderson, an Ibo scholar and historian, writes,

> Symbolically, the marketplace was defined as outside the sphere of assertion by males, whether human or animal; any cock that crowed there during trading hours must become the property of the women. The connection of men with market trade comes mainly through their individual sponsorship of their wives or daughters as traders.[64]

Men, however, were not prohibited from attending the markets. They attended. But as one historian puts it, "men sat together in their age groups, drinking and chatting, while women did the lion's share of the buying and selling."[65]

Since markets served as exchange centers for goods and services, they were considered extremely important to the lives of the women. "It was a great punishment for any woman, either by village or family sanctions, to be forbidden to go to the market," says a British missionary who lived among the Ibos for thirty-five years. "The market reflects the vitality of the Ibo society's economic life. It is intensive and dominates the life of the people to an amazing degree."[66]

Ibo market currencies were abundant and varied. They included cowrie shells, horseshoe-shaped manillas of copper and brass, brass rods, and tiny arrow-shaped pieces of iron, called the *umumu* currency. Some goods were also simply exchanged for other commodities of equal value through barter.

Market Days

The markets were held every four days, arranged around the Ibo week. (The Ibo week is four days long—*eke, orie* or *oye, afor,* and *nkwo.*) People from neighboring villages were expected to attend. Since maximum attendance and participation was desired, each

Ibo basket weavers carry their wares to the marketplace. Ibo women are renowned not only for their skillful weaving, but also for their pottery and beadwork.

village was careful to choose a day that did not conflict with the market days of its neighbors. Consequently, each village market was named for the weekday that it was held. The names contained two words, the first representing the day of the week, the second, the village's name. Examples include Nkwo Otulu, Eke Nnarambi, Afor Ogbe, Orie Ekpa.

The markets were held at a clearing in the center of the village, usually the village square, with gigantic trees for shade. At the far corner of the square, underneath a massive tree shade, was located the shrine of the market god. He was responsible for maintaining peace and safety in the market and ensuring the villagers a profitable trading day. Very early in the morning, before the start of the market session, the women's leaders poured libations and prayed to the god of the market for the protection of all attending. "Women age-sets within the village took turns keeping the marketplace clean. They also arose at dawn on market days to sweep the square, be-fore the people began to stream in at sun-rise,"[67] writes Sonia Bleeker.

The women arrived early at the market with loads of foodstuff, yams, cocoyams, cassava, maize, peppers, and fruits, as well as baskets, mats, pots, and a few livestock. "All goods and foodstuffs were set out in their appointed sections and lanes were somehow kept between them,"[68] notes Leith-Ross. Buyers knew exactly what section of the market to visit for the products they needed.

Buying and Selling of Products

Prices were never set for the goods, and people haggled in loud voices before a trade was completed. Prices asked by the sellers were always higher than those finally agreed upon. The buyer examined the items of interest to show approval or dissatisfaction. She then offered a price that was normally lower than the product's worth. Both the seller and the buyer

A Vital Economy

The market formed the center of financial activity in a traditional Ibo village. It served as the place where villagers brought their surplus goods for sale or exchange for other needed commodities. The markets were always rowdy and filled with great vitality. Ibo women took pleasure in going to the markets because it also served as an avenue for social meetings. Margaret Green describes Ibo markets in her book Ibo Village Affairs.

"If agriculture is the basic occupation of these Ibo people, trading is a close second. One might almost say that whereas they farm of

necessity, they trade not only of necessity but also for pleasure. Their markets are one of the main features of their lives. They provide a meeting point for the discussion of common business and for the dissemination of news; they are a social event where the spice of gossip, the recreation of dancing and the zest of a bargain relieve the almost continuous toil of hoeing, planting, weeding, and harvesting throughout the year. Trading is the breath of life, particularly to the women among the Ibo, and the vigor with which bargaining and haggling are conducted is evidence of the prestige attached to successful commercial enterprise."

Both buyers and sellers crowd into an Ibo marketplace in the village of Ibagwa, near Nsuka, Nigeria. Such markets were usually held in the village square and attracted customers from neighboring villages.

haggled until they reached a compromise. If they were unable to compromise, the buyer was free to try her luck with other sellers. "Generally, however, the prices of market commodities were set by supply and demand,"[69] writes Victor Uchendu. For example, the price for staple foods like yam and cassava rose in the planting season when farm produce was scarce and fell in the harvest season.

Because of the haggling involved and the need to make a good sell or purchase, Ibo women generally spent considerable time on the market scene. Often, going to the market was a whole day's event. But, in spite of the long hours spent in the market, Ibo women took pleasure in the market environment. The markets were more than a shopping place for the women. They served as a meeting point to renew acquaintances, discuss issues of common interest, gossip, as well as spread important news. A visitor to traditional Ibo society noted that the markets seem to strike one as almost incredible. It was filled with clamor as of a stormy sea beating against the banked trees. Often as I went to the market, it was never without a thrill that I caught the first murmur of sound, mounting higher and higher above the tree tops.[70]

Women kept the profits they made from selling their excess crops, pottery, and other crafts. They used the money as they saw fit, either for their own personal desires or for their family needs. Although, for most women, the profit made at the market was relatively small, the women tended to concede that "a few heads of cowries were worth having as a profit when life was on a modest scale, particularly when the gaining of them involved the pleasures of the market,"[71] writes Leith-Ross. Trading in the marketplace gave women the opportunity to express themselves. And women who excelled or became wealthy through trading were given much respect.

The fact that Ibo women combined several economic tasks, farming, making crafts, trading, cooking, and other housework sometimes made their lives stressful. They often

At a market in the eastern city of Aba, Nigeria, a buyer inspects a seller's bounty, which includes baskets overflowing with tomatoes, peppers, and onions.

Traditional Ibo Currency

showed signs of physical strain and made frequent references to the amount of work they did. "They sometimes seemed to do more work than men," says one writer. "But one, however, cannot deny the fact that earning their own money and [being] valued for playing intrinsic roles in the lives of their families and the village gave Ibo women greater freedom and control over their lives."[72] As Denise Paulme, a teacher and researcher in Africa for several years, notes, being economically independent accounted for a sense of self, independence, and confidence that one often finds among Ibo women. "Unaccustomed to relying on anyone but herself, the African woman will have no need to acquire a feeling of self-confidence, since she is already rarely without one."[73]

4 Marriage

"'Inu-nwunye' (marriage) has a foremost place in Ibo social economy. It looms upon the horizon of every maid and youth as an indispensable function to be fulfilled with as little delay as possible after reaching the age of puberty,"[74] writes G. T. Basden. Two words, however, summarize the Ibo concept of marriage: community and procreation. The Ibos believed that marriage was a community rather than an individual event. People married, not necessarily for love and companionship, but to fulfill the social obligation of maintaining the life of the community through procreation.

Restrictions and Requirements

While infant-marriage (a boy and a girl affianced at birth) was an acceptable practice in traditional Ibo communities, most marriages were between two consenting adults. "And usually, it was a long, tedious, and ceremonious process that consisted of certain laws and customs that must be observed,"[75] says an Ibo man. For example, marrying a relation up to ten generations removed was considered *nso ani* (forbidden). Marriages between people from the same village or the mother's village were also prohibited. The woman of such a marriage was believed either to be unable to conceive a child or to die when giving birth.

The groom was expected to pay a dowry for his wife and give gifts to the girl's mother and other family members, as well as to members of her peer group. The paying of a bride-price, explains the Nigerian writer Derry Yakubu, was an act that

> demonstrated the bridegroom's respect for his wife-to-be and in-laws. It was a token of gratitude and appreciation for the trouble the parents have taken to bring up their daughter. In a sense, the bride price is a pledge of value; the husband undertakes by that gesture to care for her.[76]

The bride's family was expected to reciprocate by providing their daughter with most of the items necessary to begin life as a married woman, such as cooking utensils, tools for tending her farm, and crops for planting. Rich families also provided their daughters with one or two maids to assist in carrying out household tasks.

The Parents' Decision

Because marriage was a communal event, most marriages were arranged. Even though the man and the woman involved were consulted, the decision of whom to marry rested with their parents. The marriage process and arrangements were carried out by the parents of the bride and groom.

Generally, when a girl reached the age of sixteen, she was considered ready for marriage, and thus began to take great care with her physical appearance. "The process was quite elaborate,"[77] says an Ibo woman. Special care was taken to adorn the hair. "Many hours were spent in combing, pulling and anointing it; and often, it was dressed in elaborate style according to fashion,"[78] writes Basden. The girl's body was painted with freehand designs in deep black or red, using camwood dye, or *uri*. Around the waist there was often a string of beads, or a rolled fragment of cloth studded with tiny brass bells called *jigida*. The adornment was completed with ivory bracelets. Girls with wealthy parents also wore coils of brass wire on their legs or heavy brass anklets.

The girl took pains to appear graceful, very amiable, and industrious. These were the qualities valued in a potential bride. Her family found opportunities to make her more visible in society. They sent her on errands that would take her to neighboring villages and potential suitors' family compounds. She accompanied her mother to the markets and was encouraged to attend community dances and other ceremonies.

During this period of "showing their daughter," the girl's parents entertained several suitors in their compound and eventually selected the best man for their daughter. "The process of selection took time," says Basden. "Since Ibo marriages are alliances between families, parents had to be convinced that they were choosing the right family as well as the right husband for their daughter."[79]

Before reaching a decision, some parents consulted a diviner or the village priest about the prospects for such a marriage alliance. All parents, however, traced family histories to make sure that the two families had no blood ties. They also made inquiries concerning the character of the suitor and members of his family—their social position, wealth, health, and the way that the men treated their wives. Personal characteristics sought in a man in-cluded industry, assertiveness, generosity, and "sense," or foresight *(Uche)*. A family history of madness or wife abuse was enough to reject a suitor.

The Marriage Process

As soon as parents were satisfied with their choice of a suitor, they sent word to the potential groom and his family, indicating that they were ready to begin the marriage process. The parents also told their daughter that they had chosen a husband for her. "Ibo girls rarely manifested antagonism to a marriage proposal," writes Basden. "They relied

Precolonial Ibo girls of marrying age adorned themselves with beads, tiny brass bells, and ivory bracelets to display their status. Wealthier girls, like those shown here, also wore brass rings around their legs.

on their parents' decision, knowing that their parents would make the right decision for them."[80]

A date was set for the engagement ceremony, or *Idoba mmanyi nwanyi*. At the appointed time, usually in the evening, the suitor and his family arrived, bringing with them large kegs of palm wine (the traditional African alcoholic drink). The girl's family provided the food for the event. Great care was taken during its preparation, as it constituted one of the highest expressions of a family's means and the women's prestige as good cooks.

After eating and drinking, the bridegroom's father would use idioms and proverbs to announce the reason for their visit. The bride's father reciprocated the greetings and would indicate to the groom that they expected him to fulfill all marriage rituals and pay the bride-price. "The average bride price consisted of cows, yams, goats, and cowries amounting to $200 or more depending on the social standing and personal charms of the girl,"[81] notes Basden.

During this marriage event, it was proper etiquette for the prospective groom to remain silent. His father spoke on his behalf. Generally, the groom simply nodded his head and laughed with the others when something funny was said. Before the party was dismissed, the intended bride made an appearance to welcome the guests. She shook hands with each person present and, like the groom, she too did not speak. Her appearance gave an opportunity for members of the suitor's family who had not met her before to see her and make an assessment of her features.

Why Hawks Eat Chicken

Traditional Ibo marriages were arranged by the parents in order to preserve their communal nature. To discourage the tendency to rebel against societal values and choose a mate for oneself, the Ibos made up stories that foretold the doomed nature of such marriages. Thomas W. Northcote, in Anthropological Report on the Ibo-Speaking Peoples of Nigeria, *cites the following folktale as one of many that describes the ill consequences of marrying someone outside the sanctioned process of Ibo communal marriage customs.*

"Once upon a time, a girl met a man in an open place. He said, 'I want to marry you.' She said, 'All right.' He said, 'I want to take you home.' She said, 'All right.' But she did not know that the man was an evil spirit. When they reached the man's house, the man took off his false nose, his false face, and his false hands. The girl cried and wanted to go back home. But the man-spirit wouldn't allow it. Then a hawk saw the girl crying and it had sympathy for her. So the hawk flew down, lifted the girl and carried her to the roof of her parents' house. The parents were glad to see their daughter. They offered the hawk a cow, some money, and all kinds of gifts. But the hawk gave no response. He continued to hold the girl captive on the roof. Then a little boy noticed that the hawk was staring at some chicken that were wandering in the compound. 'The hawk is looking at the chicken,' the boy shouted in excitement. Then the girl's parent offered a chicken to the hawk. The hawk took the chicken and ate. Then he let the girl go. That's why hawks eat chicken. Because a hawk brought home the girl who had married an evil spirit."

Visiting the Family

Customarily, a groom did not make the entire dowry payment at one time. It was usually spread out over several months. However, once the first dowry installment was made, the bride was required to pay a visit to her betrothed husband's home. The visit, or *iga nleta* usually lasted for sixteen days (four Ibo market weeks) and "provided the opportunity for the girl to become acquainted with the members of the family into which, in due time, she herself will be admitted," [82] writes Sylvia Leith-Ross. The groom's family also used the opportunity to judge the qualities of their new "in-law." As Basden describes,

> The girl's prospective family will comment upon her looks, her figure, her behavior and general character. On the practical side, opinions will be expressed concerning her capabilities in cooking and other items of housecraft. The native is not reserved or punctilious [overly concerned with manners] when pronouncing a verdict in such circumstances. [83]

During the visit, the girl was not allowed to cohabit with the groom. It was considered *aru* (an abomination) for the girl to be touched by her affianced husband while spending her days of *iga nleta* at his home. "Should a girl have intercourse with her fiancé or at any rate conceive by him before the marriage rituals had taken place, she would be looked down upon by her companions who would make her a [derogatory] song," [84] explains Leith-Ross. The songs often presented her as a person with loose morals, who violated community rules of behavior.

At the end of the sixteen-day visit, the girl returned to her home bearing several gifts from her husband's place. If she was happy with her stay at her husband-to-be's home, she kept the gifts. However, if she was displeased with her visit, she returned the gifts, thereby ending the marriage process. If this happened, the girl's family would return part of the dowry that had already been paid to them and then begin again to look for another husband for their daughter. It was also acceptable for the groom's family to end the marriage process if they found the girl's behavior during her visit unsatisfactory. They would ask the father of the groom to stop the marriage arrangements, for he or the bride's father could stop the wedding on demand.

Preparing for the Marriage Ceremony

"On the average, there was no fixed period between betrothal and actual marriage. The time was governed by the man's circumstances, how quickly he could pay the bride-price," says an Ibo woman. "However, the parties wanted to marry as soon as possible in order to start a family." [85] As soon as the larger part of the dowry had been paid, relatives of the bride and groom consulted and fixed a date for the wedding. The wedding date usually allowed four to six weeks for the bride to prepare herself for marriage. This was often a happy time for the bride. She was pampered and exempted from manual work. Her friends dressed her hair and painted her body with various designs of *uri*, or camwood dye. Her mother prepared her favorite dishes.

In some communities, the bride and other girls in the village preparing to be married, underwent the *nkpu*, or fattening ritual. The *nkpu* lasted for several weeks, during which the girls fattened themselves while receiving instructions about their new responsibilities as wives. "At the end of 'nkpu,'" says

Marriage was usually a grand and happy affair for the bride. In her book The Ibo of Biafra, *Sonia Bleeker, an anthropologist who had studied traditional Ibo society, describes the preparation for this occasion.*

"This time [marriage time] is usually a happy one for the girl. The girl's mother and her girl friends prepare the bride's favorite dishes. They do all the cooking and housework for her. She is bathed and her body is painted by her friends. Her hair is combed and elaborately plaited. The girls sing and dance and talk, giving advice and exchanging experiences. The young bride barely has time to think of any problems the future may bring or to worry about leaving her kin and friends as she goes to her new home."

an Ibo historian, "the fatter the girls were, the more gratified their prospective husbands."[86] To the Ibos, being robust was perceived as evidence of good health and a happy disposition. And most husbands wanted a happy, healthy wife.

The Marriage Ceremony

The wedding day was a huge village event. All members of the village and family members and friends from surrounding villages were invited. The groom arrived with several kegs of palm wine. "Whatever else he may provide, he must not fail to arrange for a plentiful supply of palm wine—this is virtually an essential to a truly native marriage,"[87] says Basden. The bride's family provided the food and the entertainment during the ceremony, which was held in the bride's home.

Before the marriage feast began, the bride was called and given a small gourd containing palm wine. She drank from it and then gave the rest to the groom. This symbolized that the girl had agreed to the marriage, that she was not being forced into a marriage she resents. The marriage feast lasted well into the night, with much drinking, eating, and dancing. "The feasting and celebration was meant primarily for the guests," says an Ibo priest. "Throughout the marriage feast, the bride and groom sat demurely side by side looking rather the picture of misery than happy beings. It was not considered good form to show any signs of joy. Indeed, it was proper for the bride to manifest signs of grief because of leaving her old home."[88]

Escorting the Bride Home

Sometime after dark, the groom was required to leave the marriage feast for his house. He left alone. The bride did not go home with her husband the day of the wedding. She was taken to her new home the following night by her unmarried female friends and relations and the young men who the husband sent to "fetch" his wife. The Ibos call this custom *idu ulo* (escorting the bride home).

The ritual was done amid singing and much fanfare. Songs celebrating the bride's beauty and her introduction to motherhood were abundant. Friends and relations presented gifts to the bride in the form of money, domestic utensils, livestock, and jewelry. Her parents also gave her yams and other food crops for planting. Girls of her age helped the bride carry her possessions and her gifts to her new home.

At the entrance of the compound, the bride was met by the women of the groom's family, who welcomed her and her entourage.

They would continue singing, dancing, eating, and drinking until her friends left. The bride was then taken to the shrine of the family ancestor. Libations were poured and prayers offered on the bride's behalf. The groom's father, presiding over the ceremony, asked for health, long life, and fertility for the new bride.

After this brief ceremony, the bride was taken into the hut of her mother-in-law. There she lived until a house was built for her, usually just before or after the birth of her first child. As one Ibo man puts it,

In traditional Ibo marriage, a wife shares her husband's bed but does not share his house. They, from the beginning, live separate lives, a testimony to the communal rather than individual emphasis of Ibo marriages.[89]

However, the new bride did acquire certain privileges. Though not sharing his house, she received the husband's prime attention. She also received gifts from people in her husband's village as a token of their love. She was given very light tasks to perform and was

A contemporary Nigerian couple poses for a photograph on their wedding day. For the traditional Ibo of Nigeria, the marriage ceremony was celebrated by the entire community as well as by family and friends from neighboring villages.

always well dressed, in the new clothes and jewelry given to her by her husband and other villagers. She was immediately considered a part of the husband's family and, in time, would gradually assume her responsibility of helping maintain the needs of the family.

The new bride was also given a portion of the family land to grow her crops. The land remained hers until she died or left the family through a divorce. As G. T. Basden notes,

> Traditional Ibo marriage was not merely a man taking to himself a wife. It was more than that; it was the bringing in of another person into the family. She was something more than a wife; henceforth she was a member of the clan, has her rightful place and shared in all things pertaining to it.[90]

Polygamy

Part of the reason women did not share the same house as their husbands was that polygamy was legal in traditional Ibo society, and most men had more than one wife. Consequently, each wife needed a house for herself and her children. As Victor Uchendu, an Ibo ethnographer, emphasizes, "Among the Ibos, married life was the normal condition for both men and women; polygamy, a symbol of high social status, was the ideal."[91] Most traditional Ibo men had two wives; those who were wealthy had up to ten or more wives.

Traditional Ibo culture has often been condemned by scholars because of its practice of polygamy. They argue that polygamy was an indication of the degraded status of Ibo women. "But seeing polygamy solely as a practice that devalued women is wrong and a misconception,"[92] states Leith-Ross. Polygamy did not degrade Ibo women. Polygamy was simply a reflection of a farming commu-

nity's needs in meeting some of its immediate demands for survival. As other scholars have pointed out, polygamy served important social and economic functions for the community, specifically for the women.

The Functions of Polygamy

"The practice of polygamy was a matter of survival for the women and the entire community,"[93] writes Margaret Green. Traditional Ibo economy was based on subsistence farming, and each family's survival depended on how much it could produce on the farms. Polygamy assured that enough children would be born to help farm and sustain the family. Since large portions of forest farmland needed to be cleared, tilled, and cultivated for proper sustenance, a man, his one wife, and few children were simply incapable of doing all the work. Those who tried it, as the people soon found out after the missionaries came, either lived in perpetual poverty or the women died in the effort to bear more and more children.

Polygamy also provided a reprieve for the women. "In fact, many women in traditional Ibo society not only condoned polygamy, they suggested that their husbands 'get' a second or third wife," states an Ibo anthropologist. "Sometimes, women even married the wives for their husbands, if the husband was hesitant or considered himself too poor to marry another wife."[94] The reasons for doing this were many. The Ibos at this time had no means of contraception. Because of their strong attachment to children, abortion was not an option. Very few women actually considered it. Consequently, having more than one wife constituted a form of family planning. Women were able to space out the birth of their children over two-to-three-year periods. This in turn ensured proper health for the women and the children. It prevented, in most cases, untimely deaths due to frequent pregnancies.

Polygamy also provided the women some rest from endless work. Considering the amount of work women had to do both within and outside the home, having more than one wife ensured that there were enough women to share the burden of housework, field work, and other responsibilities of an Ibo woman. It also meant that women had some time for themselves and their children.

Woman-Marriages

The counterpart to polygamy among the Ibos was the practice of "woman-marriages." While the traditional Ibos did not practice polyandry (a woman married to several men),

they did accept woman-marriages—a woman marrying other women in order to establish her own household. Women who married other women were called "female-husbands."

These marriages, for the most part, were not homosexual marriages. Ibo women married other women for several reasons. Some were barren women who married other women to bear children on their behalf. Others were older women who had lost all their children by death. The female-husbands adopted the children of their wives. Thus woman-marriage was a way childless women affirmed their value and secured their position in society.

Wealthy fertile women also married other women as an outward pronouncement of their wealth and independence. Such women divorced their husbands, bought land, and established their own compounds. An Ibo man describes his experiences as the son of a wealthy female-husband: "My mother was then a big trader and she needed someone to help in our house and so she married one wife after another."[95] The female-husband played the social role of father to the children of her wives. Their inheritance would come through her.

The women married to female-husbands were not devalued in any way. Woman-marriages underwent marriage processes and rituals similar to male-female marriages. Traditional Ibos considered both types of marriages vital to the survival of the community. In all marriages, women retained the freedom to leave a relationship if they felt uncomfortable, neglected, or abused.

Divorce

Divorce in traditional Ibo society was relatively easy to obtain. A man could divorce his wife for adultery and neglect. Women divorced their husbands for reasons of abuse and neglect, or if the husband was a known thief or criminal. There were no undue hardships associated with divorce. The husband was entitled to the dowry he paid for the wife, when and if she remarried. The man retained legal custody of the children and the woman had visitation rights. "Consequently, divorced women were rarely considered a burden to themselves or their families. Women, who wanted to remarry, did so freely and repaid their dowries,"[96] writes Leith-Ross. Daughters were always welcomed home. And most families went so far as to ask their daughters to return if they were involved in an abusive relationship.

Widowhood

Because women married men who were at least fifteen years older than them, most outlived their husbands. Precolonial Ibo society, therefore, had rituals that widows were expected to observe. It also had set rules to protect the well-being of a widow and her children.

When a husband died, his wives underwent a period of mourning that lasted for a year. They were expected to crop their hair, live in seclusion, and wear rags for the entire period. As Leith-Ross explains,

> They may go to market, but not to their own village market; they may farm, but they will be careful to go to their farms a little time after the others have gone out, as men do not care to meet a widow too early in the morning, lest the same fate befall them as befell the widow's late husband.[97]

At the end of the mourning period, widows underwent a cleansing ritual and were reintroduced into society.

A woman whose husband died before they could bear a child had two options. She either returned home to her parents and remarried or she married one of her husband's brothers or his oldest son by another wife. Most of the time, the men were already married. But since polygamy was allowed, adding a new wife was not a problem. The interest of the new wife was protected and she was not treated differently from the other wives.

A widow with children had several options also. She could choose to remain unmarried, stay in her husband's home, and maintain her husband's property for her chil-

The Husband's Duty

Traditional marriages had specific expectations for men and women. It was the duty of the wife to bear children and maintain the household. Victor Uchendu, an Ibo ethnographer, describes the husband's function in his book The Igbo of Southeast Nigeria.

"The husband's main duty to his wife is to provide the conditions for her to maintain a thriving and expanding household. He must provide the domestic setting in which his wife works, and furnish her with a reliable supply of major staple foods from his farms. He must allot a household garden to each wife and provide palm fruits from his trees for the domestic use and for trade. The husband is also expected to allocate his cotton crop for his wife's trade, and to give periodic trade advances in money to finance her market activities."

dren. In such a case, the husband's relatives were expected to look out for her interests and protect her rights. She could also choose to marry her husband's brother and become one of his wives. A third option was to return to her parents' home with her children. And, as long as she remained unmarried, her husband's relatives were required to provide for her. When the children came of age, they were then expected to go back to their father's home to claim their father's property.

The laws governing marriage, divorce, and widowhood in precolonial Ibo society maintained the people's communal way of life. But despite its emphasis on community rather than individual survival, there were genuine attempts to maintain equity and fairness. A woman reserved the right to reject the husband chosen for her by her parents. She could also, without many repercussions, leave a marriage she found unsatisfactory. And if she was widowed, there were established laws to protect her interests and those of her children. For the most part, traditional Ibo women had the freedom and the opportunity to decide their own fate.

Motherhood

In traditional Ibo society, the major function of a wife was to bear children. "Companionship was all fine and dandy and love was good, but a childless marriage was no marriage at all,"[98] says an Ibo woman. Denise Paulme, a teacher who lived and taught for several years in Africa, writes that Ibo "women set greater store by their children than by their husbands. For it was only by becoming a mother that they felt truly fulfilled."[99]

Traditional Ibo mothers proudly called themselves "the trees that bear fruit." The phrase emphasized their procreative powers and recognized the fact that it was through the children they bore that the survival of individual families and the future of the entire community depended. Even in contemporary society, many Ibo proverbs and phrases still express the value placed on children; for example, *Onye nwe nwa ka onye nwe ego* (A person who has children is far greater than a person with monetary wealth) and *Nwa bu uba* (A child is wealth).

Twins and Others

However, in spite of its emphasis on children, precolonial Ibo society had certain taboos regarding childbirth, such as the birthing of twins, deformed or handicapped babies, babies born feet first, or babies born with teeth. Such babies were simply thrown away into the forest because they were considered abnormal and a bad omen. "To traditional Ibos,

abnormality was the equivalent of evil," writes Professor Nwala. "Anything that seemed to deviate from the perceived natural order was seen as evidence of 'aru' or an abomination

Ibo women take great pride in motherhood, believing it is their duty to procreate for the benefit of the entire community.

committed by the parties concerned."[100] It was, therefore, the village responsibility to clear itself of such evils, punish the offenders, and purify the community.

Pregnancy

Women were expected to show signs of pregnancy soon after marriage. A bride became visibly worried if after a few months of marriage she did not get pregnant. Often, family members would also begin to worry, and several sacrifices were then offered to propitiate the gods and the spirits of influential ancestors. After several years of failed expectations, the woman could divorce her husband and try her "luck" with another husband.

If, however, a wife began to show signs of pregnancy, the family was relieved and pleased. The entire family then took steps to observe the rituals necessary for a successful pregnancy. Because of the high rate of miscarriages and infant deaths in traditional Ibo villages, the people believed in complete observance of the pregnancy rituals. Anthropologist Simon Ottenberg explains:

> The rituals included total abstinence from sexual relations. The woman must avoid places inhabited by spirits. She was expected to abstain from eating certain foods which were thought to have a harmful effect on the unborn child.[101]

In addition to observing all the pregnancy rituals, the child's father was expected to consult the village diviner who prescribed certain rules of behavior as well as herb mixtures to be used in caring for the wife. Constant prayers were offered to the gods and libations poured in honor of the spirit of the ancestors, asking for protection.

The Birth of a Child

Expectant mothers were looked after by the local midwives or older women in the family. Babies were born at home, usually in a secluded place in the family compound. In some communities, it was actually considered *aru* (an evil omen) for a child to be born in the house. Such a child suffered the same fate as twins.

The father kept away during the actual birth. "No males, not even herbalists or other male medical practitioners, were allowed to be there; the child was born into an exclusively female environment,"[102] states Ottenberg. The baby was expected to cry vigorously at birth, as this was taken as a sign of health and vitality. "An infant who did not cry at birth raised great concern. Every trick including pinching was used to induce it to cry." The umbilical cord was cut by the attending female and buried in the family courtyard. This act established the child as a member of the family. "It was also believed that burying the umbilical cord in the ground united the child with the spirits of the earth and its ancestors."[103] This was necessary to ensure success and good health for the child.

The new infant was washed with sand, and the skin was smoothed and massaged with palm oil. Some communities also put *nzu* (white clay) on the baby's skin. "The 'nzu' was believed to cool the skin and was also used as a multivocal symbol of good health, fertility, good life, and happiness," describes Uchendu. Then, the child and the mother were taken into the mother's hut, where a fire had been built for them. The mother was expected to share the same bed with the infant and to nurse it for two to three years. Until the baby was weaned, the mother was required to practice sexual abstinence. "It was believed that intercourse while nursing a child was detrimental to its health. It spoilt a mother's milk and would surely result in the child's death."[104]

A Grand Village Event

The birth of a new baby was a grand occasion for the whole village. "It evoked both joy and anxiety," says Uchendu. "The joy of the parents and others expressed the hope that the mother will not die, that the child had not been born sickly and will survive."[105] As soon as the baby was born, messages were sent throughout the village. All the women in the village then gathered at the new mother's compound to celebrate the birth of the child.

Nothing Like It

Traditional Ibo society considered children its most important asset. They were essential to the survival of the community. Men and women therefore acquired and maintained status in society through their children. As Simon Ottenberg, an anthropologist, indicates in Boyhood Rituals in an African Society, *nothing matches the importance of having children for the Ibos, especially for the women.*

"To have an offspring that survives is the most important success in an Ibo woman's life—nothing matches it. Her marriage or marriages may fail, her farms may spoil, her cooking may be terrible, she may lose money at trade, but if she has children to survive she is a full woman, with status among females and respect from men. A woman without children leaves her husband, tries another, and yet another, but has not fulfilled the ideal of womanhood."

They rubbed themselves with *nzu* and chanted intricate piercing cries called *Iti oro* (onomatopoeic shouts that have no meaning outside themselves). *Iti oro* was accompanied by a brief dance that demonstrated the women's happiness.

The father of the child consulted the village priest and diviners to inquire about the fate of the child and to know which ancestor's spirit had been reincarnated. "A parent was pleased to know that a certain relative has returned in the child; this confirmed a sense of unity in human relations,"[106] explains Sylvia Leith-Ross. With the aid of the priest, the father was required to visit the shrine of the ancestors to perform the rituals requested by the diviner. The reincarnated ancestor was said to be the child's guardian spirit, or Chi. Regular sacrifices were made to the Chi by the child or on its behalf for as long as life lasted.

In addition to consulting the diviners, it was also the father's duty to send a message to the wife's family announcing the arrival of "a new life." The person bearing the good news took along a gourd of palm wine and other gifts (about six Ibo yams and some dried fish) to show appreciation for the wife's family. On his return, he was accompanied by the wife's mother.

Pampering the New Mother

The new mother was required to undergo a period of confinement, called *ile omugwo*, based on the notion that she needed at least a month devoid of work and strenuous activity in order to recuperate. It was the prerogative of the mother's mother to take care of her daughter during this period of confinement. She resided with her daughter until the *ile omugwo* ended.

The new mother was pampered during this period. She received daily baths of warm water in which medicinal leaves had been soaked to facilitate her healing and was given frequent massages with soothing lotions and herbs. The new mother was also put on a special diet of very hot and spicy meals, laden with dried fish, but no oil. "The complete and adequate care of the new mother was perceived as being necessary to assure future pregnancies and health," [107] writes Ibo historian Victor Uchendu.

The New Arrival

The baby was also pampered during the *ile omugwo* period. He or she was the mother's only responsibility. First-time mothers obtained series of instructions on how to care for the infant from their mothers and other older women in the family. Neighbors visited, bearing goodwill and gifts for the baby. "Not to visit a new mother and baby at this time would be considered an evidence of ill-will," says Uchendu. "To come as often as possible was a mark of good neighborliness." Gifts received ranged from small bangles for the new baby to prepared food for the new mother. There was also entertainment for the visitors. "The father was obliged to show his love for his wife as well as his social status by displaying drinks and foods for all the visitors or he was met with unkind criticisms." [108]

On the eighth day, or as soon as the child's navel cord had fallen off, he or she was circumcised by a native doctor or midwife. Female circumcision was limited to clitoridectomy. The Ibos never had any religious or other reasons to justify the ritual of female circumcision. "The reason offered most for the practice was that it facilitated childbirth later in life," [109] says an Ibo woman.

The Naming Ceremony

At the end of *ile omugwo,* the much rested, and by this time robust-looking, mother prepared herself and the baby for the naming ceremony. Traditional Ibos believed that looking robust was a sign of happiness and good health. Skinny women were not appreciated. As a result, during the time of *ile omugwo* every woman made the utmost effort to look "healthy." People invariably made comments on her appearance. *Ahu di ya* meant that she looks well. *O tara ahu* and *Odika obi adighi ya nma* (She lost weight and It seems she is not happy) were considered the worst pronouncements anyone could make about a woman who had just undergone a month of pampering.

The day of the naming ceremony, *Ikuputa Nwa,* was full of activities. In the early morning, the father provided his wives (but not the child's mother) and other compound women with yams to cook for the feast. He also provided large quantities of palm wine for the event.

During the actual ceremony, the child's mother adorned herself in new clothes specifically bought and tailored for the occasion. From the compound and the community, other women, dressed in their own best, joined her as they sang songs and danced in celebration of motherhood and the changes the new child would bring to the life of the family. Some of these unique songs sung by the women included "If your mother sends you to work for her, do it!"; "Thank the person called mother. My mother may it be well with you"; and "If a woman is under nursing and the soup does not taste, then you know that she has no firewood," (that is, she cannot boil the soup well because she is not in a position to obtain firewood, as she has just given birth).

Men were present during the naming ceremony, but mainly as observers. Naming ceremonies were mostly an affair for the women. The village priest presided over the ceremony. He blessed the child and prayed that he or she may live a long, productive life. Sacrifices were made to the ancestors and at the shrine of the fertility god to thank them for the birth of the child and to ask for continued health for both the child and its mother.

Naming the Child

The child was given several names by major members of the family—the paternal grandparents, the maternal grandparents, the parents, and elderly aunts and uncles. "Names are not merely considered as tags by means of which individuals may be distinguished," says Uchendu.

All Ibo names have meanings and each name given to a child expresses either the circumstances surrounding the birth of the child, the family's wishes for the child, or, in cases of confirmed reincarnation, who the child has come back as.[110]

As in every culture, there were strictly male and female names as well as names that were not gender specific. Common male names included Chukwuemeka (God has done good), Ikechukwu (God's power), and Obinna (father's wishes). Common female names included Adaku (daughter of wealth), Nnenne (mother's mother), Nnenna (father's mother), and Onyinyechi (God's gift). Names that were not gender specific included

Naming Ceremonies

Naming ceremonies were great feasting events in traditional Ibo villages. Women powdered themselves, danced, and sang songs in celebration of a new life and the joys of motherhood. During an interview, Ulunwa Odimba-Nwaru recalls one of the songs usually sung by the women during the event.

O bu onye n'akpo mama
  (Who calls mother)

Nne mmuo
  (My mother)

O bu onye n'akpo mama
  (Who calls mother)

Nne mmuo
  (My mother)

Ife di nma k'anyi kele nne
  (It is good to thank mother)

Ayamma, Ayamma.
  (Yes, Yes.)

Nne m onye o ga diri nma
  (My mother, may it be well with you)

Ayamma.
  (Yes.)

Ife di nma k'anyi kele nne
  (It is good to thank mother)

Ayamma, Ayamma.
  (Yes, Yes.)

Nne m onye o ga diri nma
  (My mother, may it be well with you)

Ayamma.
  (Yes.)

Children are highly valued in Ibo culture. Precolonial Ibos favored large families; women often bore six to twelve children.

Ifeanyichukwu (nothing is too difficult for God), Chinyere (God's gift), Ngozi (blessing), and Uchechukwu (God's will).

The Queen of Mothers

Large families were the norm, not the exception, among traditional Ibos. An average Ibo woman bore six to twelve children in her lifetime. Seven children were considered the ideal, because the number seven meant completeness or perfection to the traditional Ibos. Women who bore more than seven children were considered exceptional, and when a woman had a tenth child, some communities performed a certain religious rite in appreci-

ation of motherhood. The ritual was called *igbu ewu ukwu*. This ritual dictated that a goat be killed to celebrate the woman's ability and strength to bear children. After the ceremony, the woman was considered a "queen of mothers." She acquired respect and status in society. People considered her rich and blessed and, most often, she was viewed as a leader of women.

Mother as Sanctuary

However, every mother, no matter how many children she had, was considered sacred and a sanctuary for her children. "Nobody in the world cares more for the good and well-being

A Place of Refuge

The traditional Ibos considered the mother's natal home as a place of refuge and protection for her children. A child was always welcome in its maternal grandparents' home, as Richard Henderson, an Ibo historian, describes in his book The King in Every Man.

"A person must maintain an active relationship with his mother's kinsmen if his life is to be at all secure. . . .For the daughter's child, the home of his mother's parents stands as an ultimate refuge. In cases of marital separation, small children remain with their mother when she returns home. If there is a killing within the patrilineage, and a person is expected to hang for it, that person may flee to the home of [the] mother's parents and find refuge there. If there are many disputes in a patrilineage, and so many people die there that the land becomes a 'fiery surface,' all members of the group may scatter to the homes of their mothers' parents. The strength of the relationship between a daughter's child and his maternal grandparents is supported by powerful religious sanctions. It is believed that major spirits of the land 'love their daughter's children.'"

of the child than its mother," the Ibos believe. Therefore, if a child who was being punished by another family member ran to his mother, it was viewed inappropriate to continue the punishment. The child considered himself safe from harm because he had found a sanctuary.

The mother's natal home (*Ikwu Nne*) also served as a sanctuary for the child. It was considered a "place of motherly indulgence," according to Richard Henderson, an Ibo historian. "The daughter's child 'can do no wrong' in the home of his mother's parents. He may enter the house and demand food, may enter a room and appropriate some object which strikes his fancy." [111] A daughter's child was called *nwa di ala* (child of the soil); the child was considered special and the mother's kinspeople, regarded collectively as "mothers," were committed to protecting the child from harm. Consequently, the home of the mother's parents functioned as a place of ultimate refuge. A person who had committed a crime needed only to find his or her way to the mother's natal home to be safe. Nobody would dare look for the individual in the mother's natal home, even though people knew it was likely that he or she would be there.

Reciprocally, daughter's children were expected to protect the interests of their mother's family. "The daughter's child must be unfailingly loyal to his 'mother,' which means that they can always rely upon him to help and support them in need," [112] writes Henderson. Daughter's children acted as peacemakers in times of intervillage conflicts and protected maternal grandparents from harm. Should a fight break out, for example, between the maternal and the paternal villages, a daughter's child would always side with the maternal village. Describing her experiences living among the Ibos, the British traveler and scholar Margaret Green writes,

A man should, in theory, be able to feel himself fairly safe in his own birth place. But it is in the native village of his mother that he really feels himself to be persona grata [a welcome person]. "I can climb up and pick their cocoa-nuts and they will not mind," said one man to me as we walked through his mother's village, and his bearing was that of one who knows that he is welcome.[113]

Even though women performed many important functions in traditional Ibo society, they were valued most for their role as mothers. Mothers preserved the life of the community through procreation. They also had the primary responsibility of protecting their children from harm. And the children in turn were expected to remain loyal to their mothers and their mothers' natal homes. As Victor Uchendu notes, "It was because of the traditional Ibos' emphasis on mothers and maternal relationships that the Ibos often say and sometimes name their children 'Nneka' (Mother is Supreme)."[114]

CHAPTER 6

Colonization

The political, social, religious, and economic lives of the Ibos changed forever when Europeans discovered and settled in Iboland from the fifteenth through the mid–twentieth century. As various historians have noted, contact with Europe and the subsequent colonization of Iboland by the British disrupted the balance of power in Ibo society and marked the beginning of the end for the traditional roles and status of Ibo women.

The British Discovery of Iboland

Iboland's first contact with the European world occurred in 1472 when a group of Portuguese traders accidentally landed in Iboland during their attempt to discover a sea route to India. One of these early visitors, the author of a navigator's guide written about 1506, described Iboland "as a land of negroes, where there is much pepper, ivory, and some slaves."[115] However, these Portuguese adventurers did not stay long in Iboland. "They bought ivory, pepper, [and] locally made textiles, which they sold elsewhere in West Africa on their way home,"[116] writes Ibo historian Elizabeth Isichei.

With the traders' return to Portugal, news about the discovery of Iboland soon traveled to other parts of Europe. And, several years later, around 1508, a group of British merchants landed in Iboland. But, unlike the Portuguese, who generally bought local materials and left, the British were interested in settling the land.

They remained in Iboland for the next four and a half centuries, from approximately 1508 to 1960. Gradually, they colonized and imposed their way of life upon the natives.

The British colonial influence and activities in Iboland can be divided into three phases. The first was the British merchants' economic exploitation of the land and its inhabitants from the early 1500s onward. The second phase was the missionary activity that began in 1841. The third and final phase was the political takeover of Iboland by the British from 1884 until October 1, 1960. The combined influence of these activities, acting singly as well as simultaneously, overwhelmed and weakened native institutions.

Economic Colonization

Why the British colonized Iboland for more than four centuries is still a topic of debate among scholars. However, most agree that it was a combination of economic gain and the spirit of adventure that brought Europeans to sub-Saharan Africa. As some of the British colonial records show, the land with its thick forests was noted for its potential to yield massive economic resources for the British, including ivory and slaves, and later, palm oil and palm kernels. According to historian Michael Okonkwo,

The British merchants who followed the Portuguese traders to Iboland were primarily preoccupied with making profits. Their activities involved a two phased economic exploitation that began with the slave trade and ended with the displacement of indigenous economy and modes of production by European trading firms.[117]

The Impact of Slavery

The first British slave ship left West Africa for the West Indies in 1518. "Inside the ship were several Ibos who had either been captured by slave raiders or kidnaped by thieves and sold for such trifles as a small mirror, beads, iron bars and liquor,"[118] describes Isichei. The Ibos tried to stop the slave trade, and they took precautions to protect their families. But apparently the precautions were not effective. Historians estimate that for the three hundred years during which the slave trade lasted (1518–1851), millions of Ibo men and women were carried off into slavery. Over twenty thousand Ibos were sold into slavery annually.

The slave trade took away able-bodied Ibo men and women from their native land

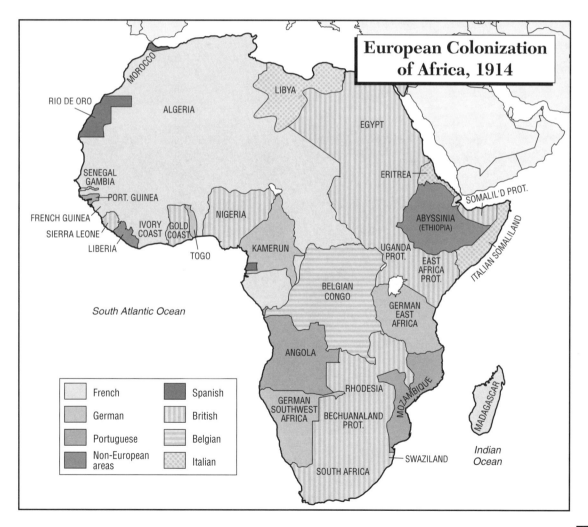

European Colonization of Africa, 1914

and terribly upset the population and the economic well-being of the people. "The slave trade robbed Iboland of many of her members, in their prime of life, and of the children they would have had," writes Professor Isichei. "We can only speculate as to the contributions they would have made to Ibo life had they remained."[119]

The effect of the slave trade, however, went far beyond the depletion of the population. It disintegrated the social bonds that had been the basis of traditional Ibo life by creating fear among the people. It also marked the beginning of the end for the village-based economy the Ibos had practiced. People were afraid to travel long distances for fear of being kidnapped. Farms in far away areas were practically abandoned. Nobody could be trusted and everyone was considered an enemy. As one former slave put it, "The whole population was continually in a state of perpetual excitement and fear. . . . Their fields were neglected. . . . Every one was afraid of his own neighbor."[120] Thus, Iboland gradually shifted emphasis from a communal-based society to a society of self-centered, fragmented lives. Since nobody could be trusted, people wanted only to protect themselves and members of their immediate families.

The Ibos' inability to engage in effective long-distance trading and productively cultivate distant farms during the slavery period put enormous strain on the lives of the women. Since long-distance trading and farming were

African slaves huddle together in the crowded quarters of a slave ship. Millions of Ibo men and women were forced into slavery between 1518 and 1851.

traditional male domains, women increasingly found themselves looked upon to provide for the family through their meager food crop production. Most women were unable to carry out this new level of economic responsibility. So the Ibos, who in their traditional society had been able to provide for themselves and their children, for the first time in their lives, began to suffer the pains of hunger and poverty.

The British government banned the slave trade in 1807. But it was not until 1851 that the slave trade was effectively stopped. "The last slave ship left West Africa for Europe in 1851,"[121] writes Isichei. By then, the economic life of the Ibos had been terribly weakened and required the combined effort of the Ibos and the British to rebuild. But, rather than helping the natives restart their native economy, the British merchants took advantage of the economic and social instability created by the slave trade and introduced the second phase of their economic exploitation—the era of big European trading companies that replaced what was left of the local economy.

The Trading Companies

At its healthiest period, the traditional Ibo method of producing food and other commodities was slow paced compared to Europe. After the slave trade, the scale of production was even smaller and slower paced. European manufacturers could produce commodities much faster and cheaper than the natives. This proved to be a profitable opportunity for the British trading companies. By mid–nineteenth century, when the slave trade was coming to an end, "there was a great influx of goods into . . . Iboland, an influx which was unprecedented,"[122] states Isichei. These imported goods from Europe competed with and quickly rivaled locally

The Social Cost of War

It is really an understatement to say that the Ibos suffered tremendously from the British invasion and the numerous wars that followed. In her book History of the Igbo People, *Elizabeth Isichei, a professor of history at a Nigerian university, describes the devastation.*

"It will be evident from the foregoing that the colonial conquest of Igboland was accomplished at great cost, both in human lives and in property. The many deaths, the looted farms and livestock, the houses razed, the trees cut down, are adequately documented even in British records, and are remembered with poignant emphasis in the traditions of the Igbo community concerned. The people of Ameke in Item [a village in Iboland] still annually observe the day in 1916, of the conflict with the British—'the blackest time of Item when one of the four principal villages was turned into a desert.'"

made products. Local craft industries such as smithing, cloth weaving, and pottery, as well as wine and beer production, were easily displaced by cheap European-made products.

The new market economy introduced by the trading companies did not particularly favor women. Although still in existence, local markets acquired a new European outlook. Women lost the monopoly they had traditionally enjoyed over the market environment, since everybody wanted a share in the new economy. And instead of being filled with products made and proudly sold by the women, a typical market by the turn of the century contained imported goods, from bicycles to canned milk, says one writer.

Even more unfavorable to the women than the changing face of the marketplace was the birth of a new gender-biased division of labor. The Ibos needed money to buy the imported goods from Europe. The trading companies, however, were not interested in buying anything from the natives, except palm oil and palm kernels. In their effort to survive, the people abandoned their emphasis on subsistence-level agriculture and began, almost exclusively, to produce palm oil and palm kernels. Men assumed the responsibility of climbing the palm trees and cutting down ripe palm fruits. The women were expected to pick the fruits, carry them home, and process the oil, which the men then took to the market. Though they played a significant role, women were not entitled to an equal share of the money obtained from the sale of the oil. They received as much as a fourth of the profit to as little as nothing, depending on the goodwill of the husband. As such, women's dependance on men increased and they were still unable to meet the needs of their families. "Thus began the relationship which condemned Ibo women to a vicious cycle of poverty and exploitation to this day,"[123] writes Isichei.

Religious and Cultural Colonization

"But, perhaps the essence of traditional Ibo life would still have been saved, had the disintegration of its economic and social life not been reinforced by missionary activities," says an Ibo man. While the merchants were busy destroying the economy of the Ibos, the Christian missionaries who came after them accomplished the breakup of the people's religious and cultural belief systems. "This they did in their zeal to convert the people to

Christianity and to show them what they supposed was 'a better way of life.'"[124]

Ironically, the first missionary activities in Iboland began in 1841 when a group of slaves who had been rescued and resettled in Sierra Leone returned to preach the Christian gospel to their people. They were soon followed by European missionaries. By 1892, Iboland was filled with many missionary organizations representing almost all major European Christian denominations—the Anglican Church, the Roman Catholic Church, the Presbyterians, the Methodists, as well as other Evangelicals. According to Elizabeth Isichei,

> The missions had much in common. They were convinced that they had a higher calling to convert the Ibo people to Christianity. They believed that they were rescuing the Ibo people from a dark world of cruel barbarism and savagery, and, by so doing, set their ways "right."[125]

The missionaries, both the returning expatriates and the Europeans, took one quick look at the Ibo people and called them "primitive." The Ibo religion, rituals, and customs they called "paganistic" and "evil." The concept of female priesthood was considered outrageous, and diviners were simply viewed as "the devil's instruments to deceive the people" and called false prophets—*Otu ndi mgbaasi* in the Ibo language. "The missionaries were hostile to Ibo religion. Not once, but repeatedly, in their writings and correspondence does one find Iboland described as the kingdom of Satan,"[126] notes an Ibo historian.

Thus, preaching their version of evangelical Christianity, male authority, and the British culture, the missionaries set about condemning and dismantling the Ibos' social and religious structures, as well as rules of established behavior. As such, female organizations were disrupted. The rituals that the Umuada (daughters of a lineage) had customarily conducted for the welfare of the families were considered "evil and satanic." Those women who joined the church, or whose husbands or brothers joined, were asked to abandon the rituals. Dancing was viewed as evil and obscene. Otu Umuagbogho (the association for young, unmarried daughters of a lineage), whose duty was to teach traditional dances to the young, was proclaimed the breeding ground for the devil.

Title-taking was viewed as paying dues to the devil and was greatly discouraged. Polygamy, the paying of a bride-price, and everything else the Ibos practiced and believed in were condemned. "The missionaries seem to have had one motto: 'everything British was good; anything Ibo was bad,'"[127] remarks an Ibo historian. The fact was that the missionaries neither understood, nor tried to understand, the native way of life.

Missionary Influence and the Mission Schools

At the beginning, converting the Ibos to Christianity was a rather difficult job for the missionaries. Between 1841 and 1900, the number of Christian converts in Iboland was estimated at a miserly 1,788. Most of the converts, according to an Ibo writer, consisted of "the poor, the needy, and the rejected: the mothers of twins, women accused of witchcraft, those suffering from diseases such as leprosy which were seen as abominable."[128] However, the progress of Christianity in Iboland underwent an astonishing transformation after 1900. In 1921, the number of Christians in Iboland was estimated at 284,835. By the 1940s, about a third of the

Hunger for Education

At the beginning of the twentieth century, many of the Ibos who had been unresponsive to the teachings of Christianity joined the church in great numbers. This was primarily due to the establishment of mission schools that gave the people opportunities for education and good employment in the new colonial government, described below by Sylvia Leith-Ross in African Women.

"The missionaries came, bringing salvation in one hand and education in the other. The people had no hunger for salvation but they were hungry for education which they saw would benefit them. Apparently education was indissolubly bound up with 'church.'

Some missions even insisted that literacy was required for baptism. The Ibo was nothing loath. Provided he acquired literacy, he did not mind being baptized: to the missionary, education was the handmaid of religion; to the heathen, religion was the means to education. They felt no need to another faith but they had great need of a new way of attaining wealth. The parents themselves often did not bother to change, but they willingly offered their children to the new God who was able, not only to unlock the gates of Heaven and Hell but, what was much more important, to open the doors of European trading firms and the desks of Government offices."

As European missionaries traveled across Africa, they established churches and schools in an effort to "civilize" the natives. Here, a Methodist minister teaches a Sunday school class in Guiongua, Angola.

Ibos (approximately 4 million) had converted to Christianity. Why did the Ibos adopt Christianity with such astonishing degree after half a century of relative indifference?

The major reason was the introduction of mission schools. By 1900, the missionaries had expanded their activities in Iboland to include the establishment of schools. "With the schools came the opportunity for formal education and employment in the new colonial government that was sweeping through Iboland like forest fire,"[129] says Leith-Ross.

The schools were not public; only church members and their children had access to them. With the fringe benefits attached, the missionary educational advantage looked very attractive. The people slowly but gradually abandoned their resistance to the "foreigners" and joined the church in multitudes. As one writer puts it, "They realized as they never did before that knowledge was power,

and that it can command a good salary."[130] Everyone wanted to have a share in the new educational opportunities. As Father Shanahan, a missionary stationed in Iboland about 1905, lamented in a letter to his superior, "All our prestige in this country comes from the fact that we are considered great educators."[131]

Gender-Biased Education

Missionary education in Iboland, however, was greatly biased, and not gender balanced. It created and fostered an atmosphere for the subjugation of women. While boys were given a regular education that prepared them for public life, girls were taught needlework, European domestic skills, the Bible, and how to be good wives and mothers. Writes author Judith Van Allen,

The missionaries' avowed purpose in educating girls was to train them to be Christian wives and mothers, not for jobs or citizenship. Missionaries were not necessarily against women. . . . Their concern was the church, and for the church they needed Christian families.[132]

Whatever their noble intentions, missionary education reinforced the notion that women were unequal and secondary to men. Women increasingly found themselves disenfranchised. Their traditional modes of power diminished as they were excluded from active participation in missionary activities as well as in the new colonial government that the British were forming.

Political Colonization

The final phase of the British colonization of Iboland began in the 1880s. This was the British political conquest of Iboland, often referred to as "the British expedition to Iboland." "Up till this point in the history of the long and complex colonial relationship between the Ibos and the British, the traditional Ibo political system was still left untouched,"[133] says an Ibo historian. The lives of Ibo women had been weakened economically and their religious beliefs and social attitudes had been shaken, but they still had the traditional political institutions that operated on the basis of separate but equal representation of men and women.

Colonial administrators in Lagos, Nigeria, meet with messengers from the interior. After colonizing Iboland, the British quickly dismantled Ibo society and subjugated women.

However, by the late nineteenth century, the British government was no longer content to have only its merchants and missionaries in Iboland. It wanted total political control. At this time in history, most ethnic groups in Africa were already under the political authority of one European nation. With its extensive trading and missionary presence in Iboland, the British thought that it would be relatively easy to make the Ibos part of its subjects. But they were wrong. It would take Britain approximately forty years of small-scale protests and massive wars to completely conquer and subdue the Ibos.

The Pacification of Iboland

When the British soldiers and officers sent to rule Iboland arrived, they found its political makeup unsuited to their needs. They had expected to find a system of government similar to that practiced in Europe and in other African ethnic groups, where one man ruled and the rest paid homage to him. Instead, what they found in Iboland were numerous democratic, independent villages that gave everyone the opportunity to participate in community life through different political organizations. "The British were surprised by the democratic nature of Ibo villages. They were even more surprised by [the] level of women's participation in politics,"[134] writes Van Allen.

The British, however, did not appreciate the Ibos' political structure. They simply regarded the political system that gave rights and representation to both men and women as irrational and ridiculous. Some colonial officers called it "primitive"; others saw it as evidence of a lack of order and discipline. They therefore began to dismantle the people's traditional political structures and introduce a system of government they thought more organized. As one colonial officer reported,

Political Disenfranchisement of Ibo Women

The British colonial officers enforced gender-discriminatory principles in Iboland. Coming from a society that did not recognize female participation in public life, the British soldiers excluded Ibo women from the colonial government, as Judith Van Allen writes in her essay "'Sitting on a Man.'"

"The experience of Ibo women under colonialism shows that Western influence can sometimes weaken or destroy women's traditional autonomy and power without providing modern forms of autonomy or power in exchange. Ibo women had a significant role in traditional political life. As individuals, they participated in village meetings with men. But their real political power was based on the solidarity of women, as expressed in their own political institutions—their 'meetings,' their market networks, their kinship groups, and their right to use strikes, boycotts, and force to effect their decisions.

British colonial officers generally failed to see the political roles and political power of Ibo women. The actions of administrators weakened and in some cases destroyed women's bases of strength. Since they did not appreciate women's political institutions, they made no efforts to ensure women's participation in the modern institutions they were trying to better."

Practically all the systems of the natives have been done away with. I call them systems for want of another word, but it would be more accurate to say that their want of systems and method has been done away with and a government organized among them.[135]

The Division of Iboland

The first thing the colonial officers did in their so-called organized government of Iboland was to ignore the independent nature of Ibo villages. They lumped all the villages under one political administration called the Southern Protectorate. Then, they joined the Southern Protectorate (Iboland) with neighboring ethnic groups and called the new creation Nigeria, meaning "the land of the Negroes."

For better control, Iboland (the Southern Protectorate) was arbitrarily divided into provinces and divisions. There were six provinces altogether, each containing about a hundred subcategories called divisions. The divisions were ruled by a select group of missionary-educated natives appointed and given authority by the British. The natives in charge of the divisions reported to a British colonial officer, or resident, in charge of their province. The resident was assisted by two or three junior officers and a number of cadets. The resident and his men were under a British governor general in charge of the entire Southern Protectorate. There were no women in the administration of the provinces or the divisions. Van Allen explains:

Thus, British imperialism submerged the democratic character of Ibo traditional politics and destroyed most of the politi-cal institutions through which women protected their interests. It destroyed women's traditional autonomy and power without providing modern forms of autonomy or power in exchange.[136]

What was left of the traditional lives of women at this time simply fell apart as a result of the British reconstruction of the political character of Ibo society. Women could no longer make policies, let alone enforce them. Decisions reached during the women's gatherings were no longer binding. For the first time in their lives, Ibo women were told what to do, and they had to obey. "They saw themselves as nonentities in the new colonial system and in the new society the British had created,"[137] says an Ibo woman. The women were not about to sit quietly and watch the colonizers ignore them and take away their political authority. To show their anger and frustration, they began a series of protests that quickly developed into what is now known as the Ibo Women's War of 1929. Although the resistance lasted for only a few months before it was crushed by the British, it marked the Ibo people's last united attempt to resist colonization and British incursion upon their lives. It is also remembered as the Ibo women's heroic and fearless confrontation against British imperialism.

The Ibo Women's War

"The Women's War movement began as a series of small localized protests organized and carried out by the women to complain about their new subservient position in Ibo society,"[138] states writer Van Allen. As stated in the official British report about the incident, the women said that they were not as happy as they were before the British came. They said that the land had changed and that they were dying. And they demanded that all white men go back to their own country so that the land might return to the way it was before the British came.

The small protests grew and culminated into large demonstrations on November 23, 1929. Ibo women living in the Aba, Owerri, and Calabar communities converged at various colonial administrative centers. They were all dressed in the same unusual way— short loincloths, faces smeared with charcoal or ashes, and heads bound with young ferns. They also carried sticks wreathed with palm fronds. This was the way Ibo women traditionally dressed when they were angry about policies and wanted some changes. "Every aspect of the women's attire symbolized distress and desperate circumstances," states historian Leith-Ross. "It was also a symbolic call to the gods for help."[139]

The women chanted, danced, and sang songs that expressed their anger and complaints. The demonstrations lasted for about six weeks, each day growing stronger and the women growing more reckless in their demands. Some women went as far as destroying or damaging anything they associated with their oppression by the British. Some broke into prisons and released prisoners, while others attacked the British courts and set fire to official buildings.

The British Response

The British colonial officials did not try to understand the women's demands, nor did they try to appease them. They saw the women's behavior as evidence of the Ibos' "irrationality and primitiveness." One British colonial officer who later reported on the event simply called them "crowds in a state of frenzy."[140]

Unsuccessful Resistance

One of the reasons the British succeeded in conquering Iboland was that they had the superior weapons of war. Elizabeth Isichei explains in her book History of the Igbo People *that the Ibos realized too late that the British had massive weapons of destruction, and what seemed like an unlimited supply.*

"The problem which faced the Igbo was that of arms and ammunition. When the British invasion of Igboland began, they discovered, too late, that the British did not themselves fight with the weapons they had sold their Igbo customers. The Igbo fought with capguns, dane guns or matchets, and the occasional rifle, and suffered from the chronic shortage of ammunition. The British fought with rifles and machine guns, and unlimited supplies of ammunition. To keep down their own casualties, they volleyed continuously into the bush as they advanced. What is astonishing, is not that Igbo resistance was unsuccessful, but that the Igbo, in the teeth of all these difficulties, resisted at all."

Facing such arrogance, Ibo women really had no chance to achieve their aim.

By mid-December, three weeks into the demonstration, the British officers at the scene felt that their lives were in danger. They sent for large numbers of police and soldiers to help stop the rebellion. The armed troops fired at the women, killing approximately fifty and injuring many more. They chased the women into the villages, burning and demolishing compounds, cutting down trees, looting farms and livestock. Properties were confiscated and fines amounting to $6,000 were levied against each village in order to pay for the damages caused during the riots.

"The shooting was on the 17th of December. Trouble continued sporadically in various parts of the disturbed area. But by the 20th the situation was completely in hand,"[141] states Professor Isichei. The Ibos never attempted any other significant resistance against British invasion after the Women's War. As one Ibo man says, "The Ibos lost heart."[142] The Women's War showed them the futility of any resistance effort. The British were better organized and better equipped and determined to carry out their mission of colonization. There was nothing the Ibos could do but accept the power and authority of the invader.

Iboland remained under British colonization until October 1, 1960, when Nigeria gained its independence from British rule. Although Britain's political withdrawal from Iboland was a peaceful process achieved by international pressure, the four and a half centuries of political, economic, religious, and social suppression of the people had taken its toll. Life as the Ibos had known it changed, and the lives of its women would never be the same.

The Modern Ibo Woman

olonialism may have brought some good to the Ibos, such as formal education and the ushering of Ibo men and women into the realm of world affairs and economy. But it threw traditional Ibo society and its system of thought into a state of disequilibrium. As one Ibo man states, "The white man took a relatively functional world and turned it upside down. The society which our ancestors had created worked for us. The new one created by the British simply does not work."[143] Modern Ibo society is simply a world of confusion, of conflicting ideals and beliefs. "The people's ultimate aim, it seems, has become a quest for individual survival,"[144] notes Ibo historian Felix Ekechi.

Political Changes

One important legacy of colonization that affects the lives of women is what the historian Nkiru Nzegwu describes as "the apathy of modern Igbo women toward political activity."[145] Contemporary Ibo society denies women active political participation. Women can vote; they can help men run for political office. But they do not hold leadership positions. "One would have expected modern Ibo women to rise up and demand their political rights the way their mothers and grandmothers had done," says anthropologist Kaneme Okonjo.

But the caliber of modern Ibo woman is different from her past ancestors. Most of them accept their secondary, subservient status without much thought. They appear unconcerned about issues with wider political and social implications.[146]

What is the reason for this sense of political apathy found among modern Ibo women? Why do they appear more politically complacent than their foremothers?

Economic Changes

Why modern Ibo women are politically apathetic may be explained by their new economic realities. When the British sent women home to be good wives and mothers during the colonial rule, they never told the women how they were to survive economically. While the men, for the most part, enjoyed their newfound public power, few were willing to take on the traditional economic responsibility of the women. Moreover, the meager income earned by men was not enough to provide adequately for the needs of the family without help from the women. Thus women, stripped of public power, barred from active and productive participation in the new economic system, still had the responsibility of feeding their children and other members of their families. "It has not been an easy task," says an Ibo mother of six. "We have no time for anything else. All we can afford to think about is how to feed our children."[147]

Comparatively, the economic life of contemporary Ibo women has regressed rather than improved since precolonial times. At least precolonial Ibo women farmed their land and were able to provide food and comfort for their family with the help of their husbands and children. Today, most women have to go it alone. Modern Ibo men, says Peter C. Lloyd, an anthropologist, "suffer a sense of dissociation from the land. They maintain an attitude of repulsion from manual work."[148] Rather than staying in their native villages to cultivate the land, they migrate to the cities and towns looking for work and supposedly better ways of life. Most of them often leave their wife (or wives) and children in the villages to fend for themselves as best they can.

For the women left in the villages (approximately half of Ibo women), life is relatively difficult. They sustain themselves through subsistence farming. "But the joys and jokes that had attended work on the farm in pre-colonial times have been replaced by worn, tired faces," says Professor T. Nwala. "Work has simply become a way of expressing life and the desire to continue living."[149]

A child bows before the king (right) and prime minister (left) of the Ibo people living in Onitsha, Nigeria. As a result of colonization, women are no longer able to hold political office.

The Modern Ibo Woman

City Life

Women who migrate to the cities and towns alone, or with their husbands, acknowledge that abandoning the agricultural life in the village does not lessen their economic hardships. Of course, those fortunate to have received formal education can live better lives, as they are able to find employment in the public sector as nurses, doctors, lawyers, and teachers. But the colonial legacy that favored men's education over women's means that relatively few women occupy these positions. The gap between men and women in the public economic sector is still very wide.

The discrepancies in education force most urban women to become self-employed. The fortunate ones acquire money from their families and start vocational businesses like tailor shops, restaurants, beauty salons, or small grocery stores. But since opening a vocational business requires huge capital, few women have the opportunity to open a business.

This leaves many women with the option of becoming petty traders. "Petty trading has become a normal feature of modern Iboland," writes Victor Uchendu. "Women hawk small items like bread, groundnuts (peanuts), bananas or fruits."[150] Some women carry the items in large trays and move from place to place in search of buyers. Others prefer to set up a table in front of their homes or on highways and sell the products to passersby. The reality for these women is that they work long hours for relatively little profit. "When the economic lives of modern Ibo women are evaluated," says Robin McKown, an anthropologist,

Today many urban Ibo women work as petty traders, selling food and trinkets to passersby.

poverty and hunger [are] a reality for many families. There is hunger in the rural villages where subsistence farming is left to women and old people. There is hunger in the cities where many workers can not earn enough money to properly feed their large families or pay for their children's school fees.[151]

The Family

The changes in the political and economic lives of contemporary Ibo women have also affected traditional family values and relationships. "The face of the Ibo traditional family has changed tremendously," states Lucy Onyekwere, an Ibo mother. "The Ibo traditional extended family unit is still recognized. But more and more Ibos are forming nuclear families."[152] This is primarily a result of the people's gradual abandonment of polygamy, condemned by the Christian faith, as well as the mass migration to the cities. Whereas in the past a typical family consisted of a man, his wives, his sons, his sons' wives, and unmarried and divorced daughters, today a typical Ibo family consists of a man, his wife, and many children.

The shift from extended to nuclear family units has created serious problems that threaten the core of Ibo society. "As men and women move to towns and focus on their single family units, their relationship with their descent groups inevitably weakens. As familial bond weakens, so does loyalty to one's family,"[153] says historian Peter Lloyd. Most Ibos express dismay at the disintegration of Ibo family life promoted by the loss of strong extended family relationships. "People have lost their sense of sharing and belonging," the Ibos complain. A newly married Ibo woman, Uchenna Adigha, describes how she has

The Disintegration of Ibo Extended Family Life

One of the legacies of colonization is the disintegration of the extended family unit. Simon Ottenberg, in "Ibo Receptivity to Change," describes how the Ibos leave their close-knit villages and move to the cities, where they eventually lose traditional family values.

"The larger unilineal descent groups [extended families], so characteristic a feature of Ibo society, are becoming less important as lineage and clan members leave home on a temporary or permanent basis, as traditional agriculture—normally under lineage and clan control—comes to play a less vital role in Ibo economy, and as belief in ancestral spirits gives way to Christianity. In turn, the importance of the smaller family groupings as social and economic units is increasing. These changes in kinship organization are most noticeable in the urban centers but are also occurring in the rural areas."

never met her uncle who lives in a city in northern Nigeria: "He did not even care to attend my wedding, even after several messages had been sent to him."[154]

The changes in the traditional family structure have not improved the social lives of Ibo women. Small families and monogamous marriages have apparent advantages, such as eliminating jealousies between co-wives and giving men and women the opportunity to develop single loving relationships. But, for the most part, the changes seem to stifle and confine women. As Christina, an Ibo grandmother, notes, "The modern marriage is a prison."[155]

Modern husbands and wives often try to combine both traditional Ibo and contemporary Western values, beliefs, and customs into their marriages.

Shifting family values have created tensions between men and women. Husband-wife relationships seem to follow a quasi-Western pattern that reflects the confusion of a people trying to mix two cultural ideals. Men seem to be uncertain about the type of relationship they want. "They try to adapt traditional values to those they have acquired through contact with the West and what results are conflicting expectations,"[156] notes Lloyd. For example, while the achievements of "an aggressive, vocal woman" are admirable, silence and subordination are promoted as ideal female behaviors. While they may respect a woman with advanced education, most Ibo men still do not want their wives to become "too educated." It is a common belief that "too much education spoils the woman and makes her uncontrollable." As an Ibo woman notes in frustration, "Present-day Ibo society does not know what it expects from its women. It gives conflicting messages."[157]

Divorce and Widowhood

Shifting values have also affected the Ibos' attitude toward divorce and the treatment of widows. In traditional Ibo society, women were free to leave a relationship they found unsatisfactory for reasons such as abuse or abandonment, and there were no undue hardships associated with divorce. Daughters were always welcomed home, with families regularly asking their daughters to return if they were involved in abusive relationships. Present-day Ibo society, however, frowns upon divorce, arguing that it goes against the law of God. Upon marriage, families simply tell their daughters "not to bother coming back."

"The negative stigma currently attached to divorce forces many women to remain in unhealthy relationships," says an Ibo woman. "Those who are courageous enough to get a divorce are ostracized by both society and their own family members."[158] They are severely punished. The husband who, in most cases, is angry that his wife left punishes her by forbidding her from seeing her children or having any relationship with them. Society punishes her as well. If she occupies any position in the church or in society, the position is taken away. She is considered an aberration and will almost never remarry. "Such negative repercussions make most modern-day Ibo women choose to endure the abuses of an unhappy marriage rather than incur public outrage,"[159] notes an Ibo woman.

The life of a widow is not much better than that of a divorced woman. Most of the traditional laws that protected the rights and property of a widow and her children are now practically obsolete. With a new sense of individualism and lack of family loyalty created by the changes in the family structure, most Ibo men are becoming rather selfish, selfish enough to appropriate their brother's

A Wonderful Heritage

Eze Akanu Ibiam, an eminent statesman and former governor of Eastern Nigeria, supports the idea of going back to rediscover the Ibo heritage as a way of building the bridge to the future and remedying the chaotic social, economic, and political conditions of lives in present-day Iboland. The following is an address given at a workshop on Ibo culture held at the University of Nigeria Nsukka. It is excerpted from Felix K. Ekechi's book Tradition and Tranformation in Eastern Nigeria.

"At a time when [peoples] the world over . . . are deeply conscious of their own particular lifestyles, their peculiar identities, and dignity, it is my avid hope that [the Ibos] will bring to the forefront . . . the variety of ways of living which marked our forefathers as men and women of sagacity, great intelligence, foresight, and outstanding courage.

We have lost a good deal of the wonderful heritage which our fathers built up and left behind for us. We are now a mixed group of Christians and non-Christians. We are composed of literates and illiterates. There are the very rich and very poor. Our beautiful and praiseworthy extended family system is crashing and might finally become a thing of the past, if we do not wake up to our blessed responsibilities. It is incumbent upon all Ibo men and women to reclaim their heritage, to work toward the revival of Ibo culture."

property and deny the widow and her children their property rights.

A widow with children often finds herself fighting with her husband's brothers to protect her interests and those of her children. The life of a widow is difficult. She is often alone in her struggles and, unless she is strong and diligent, she will become destitute. Although people outside her husband's family feel sympathetic toward her, and marrying a widow does not carry the same stigma as marrying a divorced woman, she will most often not remarry. Not many men want to deal with the problems and family squabbles a widow inevitably brings to a relationship.

A Revival of Traditional Ibo Values

With the obvious economic and social instabilities in the lives of contemporary Ibos, many have begun to ask whether the Ibos are not better off going back to reclaim their past. There is a strong belief among concerned Ibo men and women that reinstating traditional rituals and customs destroyed during the British contact will bring balance and restore the Ibos' sense of cultural identity.

These voices argue that if the Ibos are to make progress for themselves and their children, they must first rediscover their history. They must have a basis upon which to stand and build the future. In an address given by a former Nigerian head of state, General Obasanjo, he asked the people, "Should we not, in our own interest and in the interest of humanity, hark back to our traditions of 'esprit de corps' and communalism and build an economy and a society of our own?"[160] General Obasanjo was convinced that the only way the people can succeed in creating a better life for themselves and their children is to

revamp the rapidly disappearing traditional values and beliefs.

In the wake of the revivalist movement, many Ibo communities have begun to reinstate traditional female political associations. Some communities have reestablished the position of the Omu (the women's spiritual and political leader). Kaneme Okonjo, an Ibo, describes how a new Omu was recently reinstalled in the Oguashi Ibo community.

It was the first such event in the town since independence. After the long period of non-recognition of the Omu during the colonial era, a renewed spirit of loyalty to her and support of her role is readily apparent in the community.[161]

Although greatly discouraged by Christian churches, many women have begun to take traditional titles. In some communities, like that of Otulu Mbaise in Imo State, many of the traditional female social groups are making a comeback. Several community-based women groups have formed and are participating actively in the development and management of community affairs.

A House Divided

But there are problems with this crusade to reclaim the past. The movement is not widespread. Some Ibos see the effort as wasted. They argue that "no generation can ever succeed in reviving any culture in its entirety."[162] Moreover, they contend that there are certain traditional practices, like the killing of twins, that the Ibos are better off without. "What the Ibos need today and in the future," quotes Ekechi, "is to be selective and practical. The Ibos should examine their traditional customs and cultures closely and determine which aspects should be revived and which should be discarded."[163] The question that remains to be answered, however, is Who makes the decision? Who has the ultimate authority to decide which customs should be revived and which should be discarded? Ibo men and women today have diverse interests, education, ambitions, and ways of life. This makes it extremely difficult, if not impossible, to unite and achieve one goal.

On the far end of the debate, however, are those who question the efficacy of going back to what is past. Ekechi quotes one critic as saying, "The world is changing fast. The Ibos are better off marching with the tunes of the time, looking to the future and not to the past."[164] This group contends that the Ibo society has made major gains in increasing the standard of living since its independence from British rule. "We must prevent a reversal of our major gains," they assert. "The prospects for success are brighter now than ever before and we must not relent in our efforts."

As one of the leaders of Iboland, the late Dr. Nnamdi Azikiwe, remarks, "No nation can grow out of chaos."[165] Things in current Iboland look quite chaotic. One wonders how the people can prosper by rejecting their traditions. One also wonders whether there can be a future without an appreciation and recognition of the past. But the verdict as to which way Iboland should go is still out. The questions of what the future holds for modern Ibo women and where they see themselves in the twenty-first century are still being asked, with no solid answers given.

The Future

There is no question that contemporary Ibo society regards its women as secondary citizens. "They are denied the right to self-representation and treated like minors," says Nkiru Nzegwu, an Ibo woman. "Their economic lives are anything but pleasant."[166] But how long Ibo women will remain disenfranchised and what the future holds for them are still questions to be answered. Felix K. Ekechi, an Ibo professor of history, reminds that "as with cultures of the rest of the world, Ibo culture is not static, but prone to change, and changing fast."[167] Anything can happen.

The Road Not Taken

Modern Ibo boys and girls believe that the way to a good life is by abandoning traditional values and borrowing from the West. To them, progress and civilization are equated with Western values. Their views are well expressed in this poetic extract from the "Song of Ocol" by Okot p'Bitek. The complete poem can be found in p'Bitek's Song of Lawino and Song of Ocol.

Bid farewell
To your ancestral spirits
Fleeing from the demolished Homestead,
With their backs to you
They can no longer hear
Your prayers,
Waste no more chicken or goat
   Or sheep
As sacrifices to them,
They are gone with the wind
Blown away with the smoke
Of the burnt Homestead!
Stop crying
You woman,
Do you think those tears

Can quench the flames
Of civilization?
Wash your face with cold water
Here's soap and towel
Take some aspirin
It'll clear your headache
I see the great gate
Of the City flung open.
I see men and women
Walking in . . .

And what are you doing there
Under the tree
Why don't you walk in
With the others?
Are you homesick
For the deserted Homestead?
Or are you frightened
Of the new City?

You have only two
Alternatives, My sister,
Either you come in
Through the City Gate
Or take the rope and hang yourself!

As the modern Ibo woman grapples for a place in society, she must determine whether to embrace the legacy of her foremothers while forging her own future.

Even more significant to the future of Ibo women and society are the challenges and pressures the new generation of young Ibo women are exerting. The generation of girls who will mature and become Ibo women at the turn of the twenty-first century want better lives than those of their mothers; they have different expectations of married life and different views of life in general. "They insist that they want balanced, stable and fulfilling lives, equality with men and greater participation in the political life of the society," states Ulunwa Odimba-Nwaru, an Ibo mother of three girls. "When one talks with them, one sees a determination to succeed where their mothers have failed." [168]

The discussion concerning the need to revive traditional Ibo values seems to be lost on this generation. "Young men and women are often intolerant and impatient of traditional ways and values. A few are ashamed of them," writes Peter Lloyd, a historian. "They equate success and civilization with westernism and are quick to borrow whatever comes their way." [169] "But all hope is not lost," says an editorial in a recent West African newspaper. "What the future holds still remains to be seen." [170] As the Ibos say, *"Echi di omirimi"* (The future is too deep), and *"Ka ndu di,"* (Let there be life). Embedded in the phrases are feelings of hope and possibility.

Notes

Introduction: Women in Transition

1. Sylvia Leith-Ross, *African Women: A Study of the Ibo of Nigeria.* New York: Praeger, 1965.
2. Lord Frederick Lugard, foreword to Leith-Ross, *African Women.*
3. Felix K. Ekechi, *Tradition and Transformation in Eastern Nigeria.* Kent, OH: Kent State University Press, 1989.
4. Jack Harris, "The Position of Women in a Nigerian Society," *Transactions of the New York Academy of Sciences,* vol. 1, January 1940.
5. Carolyne Dennis, "Women and State in Nigeria: The Case of the Federal Military Government, 1984–5," in Haleh Afshar, ed., *Women, State, and Ideology: Studies from Africa and Asia.* Albany: State University of New York Press, 1987.
6. Harris, "The Position of Women in a Nigerian Society."

Chapter 1: The Ibo Society

7. Derry Yakubu, *African Cultural Heritage.* East Lansing: Michigan State University, 1980.
8. Leith-Ross, *African Women.*
9. G. T. Basden, *Niger Ibos.* New York: Barnes & Noble, 1966.
10. Leith-Ross, *African Women.*
11. Sonia Bleeker, *The Ibo of Biafra.* New York: William Morrow, 1969.
12. T. Uzodinma Nwala, *Igbo Philosophy.* Ikeja, Lagos: Litermed Publications, 1985.
13. Simon Ottenberg, "Ibo Receptivity to Change," in William R. Bascom and Melville J. Herskovits, eds., *Continuity and Change in African Cultures.* Chicago: University of Chicago Press, 1959.
14. Quoted in Elizabeth Isichei, *A History of the Igbo People.* New York: St. Martin's Press, 1976.
15. Leith-Ross, *African Women.*
16. Yakubu, *African Cultural Heritage.*
17. Quoted in Isichei, *A History of the Igbo People.*
18. Quoted in Isichei, *A History of the Igbo People.*
19. Isichei, *A History of the Igbo People.*
20. Basden, *Niger Ibos.*
21. Victor C. Uchendu, *The Igbo of Southeast Nigeria.* New York: Holt, Rinehart & Winston, 1965.
22. Yakubu, *African Cultural Heritage.*
23. Quoted in Isichei, *A History of the Igbo People.*
24. Isichei, *A History of the Igbo People.*
25. Quoted in Isichei, *A History of the Igbo People.*
26. Nwala, *Igbo Philosophy.*
27. Nwala, *Igbo Philosophy.*
28. Nwala, *Igbo Philosophy.*
29. Uchendu, *The Igbo of Southeast Nigeria.*

Chapter 2: Women of Power

30. Kaneme Okonjo, "The Dual-Sex Political Systems in Operation: Igbo Women and Community Politics in Midwestern Nigeria," in Nancy J. Hafkin and Edna G. Bay, eds., *Women in Africa.* Stanford, CA: Stanford University Press, 1976.
31. Leith-Ross, *African Women.*
32. Okonjo, "The Dual-Sex Political Systems in Operation."

33. Okonjo, "The Dual-Sex Political Systems in Operation."
34. Ulunwa Odimba-Nwaru, interviews with author, June 1996–January 1997.
35. Ikenna Nzimiro, *Studies in Ibo Political Systems*. Berkeley and Los Angeles: University of California Press, 1972.
36. Odimba-Nwaru, interview.
37. Margaret Green, *Ibo Village Affairs*. New York: Praeger, 1964.
38. Leith-Ross, *African Women*.
39. Harris, "The Position of Women in a Nigerian Society."
40. Harris, "The Position of Women in a Nigerian Society."
41. Green, *Ibo Village Affairs*.
42. Harris, "The Position of Women in a Nigerian Society."
43. Nzimiro, *Studies in Ibo Political Systems*.
44. Isichei, *A History of the Igbo People*.
45. Nzimiro, *Studies in Ibo Political Systems*.
46. Isichei, *A History of the Igbo People*.
47. Nzimiro, *Studies in Ibo Political Systems*.
48. Nzimiro, *Studies in Ibo Political Systems*.
49. Nzimiro, *Studies in Ibo Political Systems*.
50. Isichei, *A History of the Igbo People*.

Chapter 3: Women's Work

51. Bleeker, *The Ibo of Biafra*.
52. Basden, *Niger Ibos*.
53. Leith-Ross, *African Women*.
54. Yakubu, *African Cultural Heritage*.
55. Barry Floyd, *Eastern Nigeria*. New York: Praeger, 1969.
56. Daryll Forde and G. I. Jones, *The Ibo and Ibibio-Speaking Peoples of South-Eastern Nigeria*. London: International African Institute, 1967.
57. Leith-Ross, *African Women*.
58. Uchendu, *The Igbo of Southeast Nigeria*.
59. Nwala, *Igbo Philosophy*.
60. Quoted in Isichei, *A History of the Igbo People*.
61. Quoted in Isichei, *A History of the Igbo People*.
62. Quoted in Isichei, *A History of the Igbo People*.
63. Basden, *Niger Ibos*.
64. Richard N. Henderson, *The King in Every Man*. New Haven, CT: Yale University Press, 1972.
65. Bleeker, *The Ibos of Biafra*.
66. Basden, *Niger Ibos*.
67. Bleeker, *The Ibos of Biafra*.
68. Leith-Ross, *African Women*.
69. Uchendu, *The Igbo of Southeast Nigeria*.
70. Leith-Ross, *African Women*.
71. Leith-Ross, *African Women*.
72. Green, *Ibo Village Affairs*.
73. Denise Paulme, ed., *Women of Tropical Africa*. Berkeley and Los Angeles: University of California Press, 1974.

Chapter 4: Marriage

74. Basden, *Niger Ibos*.
75. Uchendu, *The Igbo of Southeast Nigeria*.
76. Yakubu, *African Cultural Heritage*.
77. Odimba-Nwaru, interview.
78. Basden, *Niger Ibos*.
79. Basden, *Niger Ibos*.
80. Basden, *Niger Ibos*.
81. Basden, *Niger Ibos*.
82. Leith-Ross, *African Women*.
83. Basden, *Niger Ibos*.
84. Leith-Ross, *African Women*.
85. Odimba-Nwaru, interview.
86. Basden, *Niger Ibos*.
87. Basden, *Niger Ibos*.

88. Basden, *Niger Ibos.*
89. Professor Michael Okonkwo, interviews with author, June 1996–January 1997.
90. Basden, *Niger Ibos.*
91. Uchendu, *The Igbos of Southeast Nigeria.*
92. Leith-Ross, *African Women.*
93. Green, *Ibo Village Affairs.*
94. Uchendu, *The Igbo of Southeast Nigeria.*
95. Uchendu, *The Igbo of Southeast Nigeria.*
96. Leith-Ross, *African Women.*
97. Leith-Ross, *African Women.*

Chapter 5: Motherhood

98. Odimba-Nwaru, interview.
99. Paulme, *Women of Tropical Africa.*
100. Nwala, *Igbo Philosophy.*
101. Simon Ottenberg, *Boyhood Rituals in an African Society: An Interpretation.* Seattle: University of Washington Press, 1989.
102. Ottenberg, *Boyhood Rituals in an African Society.*
103. Uchendu, *The Igbo of Southeast Nigeria.*
104. Uchendu, *The Igbo of Southeast Nigeria.*
105. Uchendu, *The Igbo of Southeast Nigeria.*
106. Leith-Ross, *African Women.*
107. Uchendu, *The Igbo of Southeast Nigeria.*
108. Uchendu, *The Igbo of Southeast Nigeria.*
109. Odimba-Nwaru, interview.
110. Uchendu, *The Igbo of Southeast Nigeria.*
111. Henderson, *The King in Every Man.*
112. Henderson, *The King in Every Man.*
113. Green, *Ibo Village Affairs.*
114. Uchendu, *The Igbo of Southeast Nigeria.*

Chapter 6: Colonization

115. Quoted in Isichei, *A History of the Igbo People.*
116. Isichei, *A History of the Igbo People.*
117. Okonkwo, interview.
118. Isichei, *A History of the Igbo People.*
119. Isichei, *A History of the Igbo People.*
120. Quoted in Isichei, *A History of the Igbo People.*
121. Isichei, *A History of the Igbo People.*
122. Isichei, *A History of the Igbo People.*
123. Isichei, *A History of the Igbo People.*
124. Okonkwo, interview.
125. Isichei, *A History of the Igbo People.*
126. Isichei, *A History of the Igbo People.*
127. Okonkwo, interview.
128. Isichei, *A History of the Igbo People.*
129. Leith-Ross, *African Women.*
130. Isichei, *A History of the Igbo People.*
131. Quoted in Isichei, *A History of the Igbo People.*
132. Judith Van Allen, "'Sitting on a Man': Colonialism and the Lost Political Institutions of Ibo Women," *Canadian Journal of African Studies*, vol. 6, 1971.
133. Okonkwo, interview.
134. Van Allen, "'Sitting on a Man.'"
135. Quoted in Isichei, *A History of the Igbo People.*
136. Van Allen, "'Sitting on a Man.'"
137. Odimba-Nwaru, interview.
138. Van Allen, "'Sitting on a Man.'"
139. Leith-Ross, *African Women.*
140. Quoted in Leith-Ross, *African Women.*
141. Isichei, *A History of the Igbo People.*
142. Okonkwo, interview.

Chapter 7: The Modern Ibo Woman

143. Okonkwo, interview.
144. Ekechi, *Tradition and Transformation in Eastern Nigeria.*
145. Nkiru Nzegwu, "Recovering Igbo Traditions: A Case for Indigenous Women's

Organizations in Development," in Martha Nussbaum and Jonathan Clover, eds., *Women, Culture, and Development: A Study of Human Capabilities.* Oxford: Clarendon Press, 1995.

146. Okonjo, "The Dual-Sex Political Systems in Operation."
147. Victoria Nnaji, interviews with author, September–November 1996.
148. Peter C. Lloyd, *Africa in Social Change.* New York: Praeger, 1968.
149. Nwala, *Igbo Philosophy.*
150. Uchendu, *The Igbo of Southeast Nigeria.*
151. Robin McKown, *The Colonial Conquest of Africa.* New York: Franklin Watts, 1971.
152. Lucy Onyekwere, interviews with author, December 1996–January 1997.
153. Lloyd, *Africa in Social Change.*
154. Uchenna Adigha, interview with author, June 1996.
155. Quoted in Leith-Ross, *African Women.*
156. Lloyd, *Africa in Social Change.*
157. Onyekwere, interview.
158. Odimba-Nwaru, interview.
159. Odimba-Nwaru, interview.
160. Quoted in Ekechi, *Tradition and Transformation in Eastern Nigeria.*
161. Okonjo, "The Dual-Sex Political Systems in Operation."
162. Ekechi, *Tradition and Transformation in Eastern Nigeria.*
163. Quoted in Ekechi, *Tradition and Transformation in Eastern Nigeria.*
164. Quoted in Ekechi, *Tradition and Transformation in Eastern Nigeria.*
165. Quoted in "Dr. Azikiwe's Legacy," editorial, *West Africa,* May 20–26, 1996.

Epilogue: The Future

166. Nzegwu, "Recovering Igbo Traditions."
167. Ekechi, *Tradition and Transformation in Eastern Nigeria.*
168. Odimba-Nwaru, interview.
169. Lloyd, *Africa in Social Change.*
170. "Nigeria at 36," editorial, *West Africa,* September/October 1996.

For Further Reading

Chinua Achebe, *Things Fall Apart,* exp. ed. Oxford: Heinemann Educational Publishers, 1996. This is the newest edition of the internationally acclaimed novel that describes life in traditional Ibo society and how the coming of the British changed the lives of the people.

Ivonne Ayo, *Africa.* New York: Knopf, 1995. Gives good illustrated descriptions of life in precolonial and present-day Africa, including a section on life in Nigeria.

Buchi Emecheta, *The Joys of Motherhood.* Portsmouth, NH: Heinemann, 1994. Traces the lives of two generations of Ibo women—the life of the mother in traditional Ibo society and how life changed for her daughter after the British came.

A. T. Grove, *Africa.* London: Oxford University Press, 1978. Easy-to-read descriptions of various geographical regions of Africa and the lives of the people in those areas.

Johanna Hurwitz, ed., *A Word to the Wise: And Other Proverbs.* New York: Morrow Junior Books, 1994. Contains some Ibo proverbs and their meanings.

Elizabeth Isichei, *The Ibo People and the Europeans.* New York: St. Martin's Press, 1973. Gives a fascinating description of life in Iboland before and after the British colonial encounter.

Colleen Lowe Morna, "Women," *Africa Report,* vol. 40, no. 1, January/February 1995. Offers a good discussion of the conflicts between the traditional and modern ways of life in African societies.

Ifeoma Onyefulu, *Ogbo: Sharing Life in an African Village.* San Diego: Gulliver Books, 1996. A simple but effective account of how the age grades function in a traditional Ibo village.

Dympna Ugwu-Oju, *What Will My Mother Say?: A Tribal African Girl Comes of Age in America.* Chicago: Bonus Books, 1996. Gives a vivid and fascinating account of an Ibo woman struggling to face the challenges of living in a changing Ibo world.

Works Consulted

Haleh Afshar, ed., *Women, State, and Ideology: Studies from Africa and Asia*. Albany: State University of New York Press, 1987. Essays that describe the political and economic status of women in Africa and Asia.

Arthur S. Banks et al., eds., *Political Handbook of the World 1995–1996*. Binghamton, NY: CSA Publications, 1996. Provides useful statistics.

William R. Bascom and Melville J. Herskovits, eds., *Continuity and Change in African Cultures*. Chicago: University of Chicago Press, 1959. Contains several essays on how African peoples have responded to the changes brought about by colonization.

G. T. Basden, *Niger Ibos*. New York: Barnes & Noble, 1966. An account of the author's thirty-five-year experience living among the Ibos.

Sonia Bleeker, *The Ibo of Biafra*. New York: William Morrow, 1969. An easy-to-read overview of life in a traditional Ibo village.

Michael Crowder, *The Story of Nigeria*. London: Faber & Faber, 1962. After studying in Britain, Michael Crowder was the first freed slave to return to Nigeria. He became archbishop of the Niger Diocese. This book details his perception of life in Iboland before and after the British invasion and colonial rule.

Felix K. Ekechi, *Tradition and Transformation in Eastern Nigeria*. Kent, OH: Kent State University Press, 1989. An overview of the changes present-day Ibo society has undergone because of colonialism.

Barbara Entwisle and Catherine M. Coles, "Demographic Surveys of Nigerian Women," *Signs*, vol. 15, Winter 1990, pp. 259–61. Gives a useful overview of the different aspects of women's life in modern Nigeria.

Nkoli N. Ezumah and Catherine M. Di Domenico, "Enhancing the Role of Women in Crop Production: A Case Study of Igbo Women in Nigeria," *World Development*, vol. 23, 1995, pp. 1731–44. Gives a good description of the economic lives of contemporary Ibo women.

Barry Floyd, *Eastern Nigeria*. New York: Praeger, 1969. Focuses on describing the geography of Iboland and its impact on the lives of the people.

Daryll Forde, *Peoples of the Niger-Benue Confluence*. London: International African Institute, 1955. Anthropological accounts of the Ibos in the traditional society.

Daryll Forde and G. I. Jones, *The Ibo and Ibibio-Speaking Peoples of South-Eastern Nigeria*. London: International African Institute, 1967. Anthropological description of the customs and rituals of traditional Ibo society.

Brenda-Lu Forman and Harrison Forman, *The Land and People of Nigeria*. New York: J. B. Lippincott, 1964. Offers a dated but good comparison of the lives of Ibo women with those of women in other ethnic groups in Nigeria.

Margaret Green, *Ibo Village Affairs*. New York: Praeger, 1964. Offers an experiential account of the lives of Ibo women after the Women's War.

Nancy J. Hafkin and Edna G. Bay, eds., *Women in Africa*. Stanford, CA: Stanford University Press, 1976. Contains several essays on different aspects of the lives of African women.

Jack Harris, "The Position of Women in a Nigerian Society," *Transactions of the New York Academy of Sciences,* vol. 1, January 1940, pp. 141–48. Describes the author's experiences during his field research in Iboland.

Richard N. Henderson, *The King in Every Man.* New Haven, CT: Yale University Press, 1972. Good description of how the women's political organizations functioned in traditional Ibo society.

Elizabeth Isichei, *A History of the Igbo People.* New York: St. Martin's Press, 1976. A detailed history of the Ibos and what happened after their contact with the Western world.

Sylvia Leith-Ross, *African Women: A Study of the Ibo of Nigeria.* New York: Praeger, 1965. An experiential account of the lives of Ibo women after the Women's War of 1929.

Peter C. Lloyd, *Africa in Social Change.* New York: Praeger, 1968. A detailed exploration of some of the changes that have taken place in African societies since the colonial rule.

Robin McKown, *The Colonial Conquest of Africa.* New York: Franklin Watts, 1971. A good introduction on the topic of how and why Europe colonized Africa and the aftermath of the colonial experience.

Helen Chapin Metz, ed., *Nigeria: A Country Study.* Washington, DC: Federal Research Division, 1992. General overview of life in Nigeria.

Nigeria Federal Office of Statistics (Lagos, Nigeria). *Annual Abstract of Statistics.* Bethesda, MD: 1991. Provides useful statistics.

Thomas W. Northcote, *Anthropological Report on the Ibo-Speaking Peoples of Nigeria.* Parts 1 and 4. New York: Negro University Press, 1969. Good description of life in traditional Ibo society.

Philip O. Nsugbe, *Ohaffia: A Matrilineal Ibo People.* Oxford: Clarendon Press, 1974. Good description of the lives of women in the Ohaffia society, where the mode of inheritance is matrilineal.

Martha Nussbaum and Jonathan Clover, eds., *Women, Culture, and Development: A Study of Human Capabilities.* Oxford: Clarendon Press, 1995. Provides detailed analysis of the economic and political development of women in third world countries.

T. Uzodinma Nwala, *Igbo Philosophy.* Ikeja, Lagos: Litermed Publications, 1985. Discusses traditional Ibo beliefs and attitudes.

Ikenna Nzimiro, *Studies in Ibo Political Systems.* Berkeley and Los Angeles: University of California Press, 1972. Good description of the political and social roles of women in traditional Ibo society.

Denise Paulme, ed., *Women of Tropical Africa.* Berkeley and Los Angeles: University of California Press, 1974. Contains several essays on different aspects of the lives of African women.

Victor C. Uchendu, *The Igbo of Southeast Nigeria.* New York: Holt, Rinehart & Winston, 1965. A general description of life in Iboland just before its independence from British rule in 1960.

Judith Van Allen, "'Sitting on a Man': Colonialism and the Lost Political Institutions of Ibo Women," *Canadian Journal of African Studies,* vol. 6, 1971. Provides analysis of women's political conditions in precolonial Ibo society. Also gives a good account of the Ibo Women's War.

Derry Yakubu, *African Cultural Heritage.* East Lansing: Michigan State University, 1980. An easy-to-read description of the major ethnic groups in Africa and their heritage.

Index

Picture Credits

Cover photo: Ifeoma Onyefulu
Paul Almasy/© Corbis, 22, 24, 76
© Peter Buckley/Photo Researchers, Inc., 16,
    19, 29, 36, 38 (top), 41, 75
Courtesy the Embassy of Nigeria, 78
FPG International, 15, 32, 45
Kerstin Geier; ABPL/Corbis, 49

Hulton Getty/Tony Stone Images, 69
Library of Congress, 64
Ifeoma Onyefulu, 11, 33, 54, 59, 83
Bioye Oyewande, 28, 42
UPI/Corbis-Bettmann, 39, 68
© Werner Forman/Corbis, 38 (bottom)

About the Author

Salome C. Nnoromele was born and raised in Nigeria. Most of her adult life, however, has been spent in the United States. She received her B.A. in English and French from the University of Utah, and her master's and Ph.D. in English and African literatures from the University of Kentucky. Currently, she is an assistant professor of English at Eastern Kentucky University.

Dr. Nnoromele is an accomplished storyteller who for many years has visited schools and libraries sharing stories about Nigeria and Africa. She has also published several essays on the subject of Africa. She strongly believes that the world must be presented with accurate pictures of Africa and its peoples. To achieve this requires that the stories of Africa and its peoples be preserved, told, and passed on to future generations.

Dr. Nnoromele lives with her husband and three children in Richmond, Kentucky.